Raising Ducks

The Ultimate Guide to Healthy Duck Keeping for Eggs, Meat, and Companionship with Tips on Choosing the Right Breed and Building the Coop for Beginners

Table of Contents

INTRODUCTION...1
CHAPTER 1: THE BENEFITS OF RAISING DUCKS 3
CHAPTER 2: UNDERSTANDING DUCK BEHAVIORS 13
CHAPTER 3: CHOOSING THE RIGHT BREED OF DUCK..........................23
CHAPTER 4: HOUSING YOUR DUCKS..36
CHAPTER 5: DUCK NUTRITION: WHAT TO FEED THEM 49
CHAPTER 6: DUCK HEALTH AND WELLNESS 63
CHAPTER 7: THE BEAUTY OF THE DUCK EGG 74
CHAPTER 8: ETHICAL CONSIDERATIONS AND BEST PRACTICES 88
CHAPTER 9: INTEGRATION, COMPANIONSHIP, AND BREEDING 98
CHAPTER 10: CHALLENGES, SOLUTIONS AND FAQS............................107
CONCLUSION..118
HERE'S ANOTHER BOOK BY DION ROSSER THAT YOU MIGHT
LIKE..120
REFERENCES 121

Introduction

When you imagine a typical homesteading scene, you'd probably think of a few animals, like chickens or cows, taking the spotlight. Rarely do you ever see ducks and geese. Why not, though? Just imagine happy little ducks splashing around in a little pond. Who wouldn't want that?

If you've ever dreamed of having your very own small farm, the idea of raising chickens might have crossed your mind. Chickens are commonly chosen for their eggs and companionship, but have you ever considered adding ducks to the mix? Ducks can be an exciting and rewarding addition to your farm, and they offer a unique set of benefits and joys that might surprise you.

One of the most delightful aspects of raising ducks is their egg production. Ducks are known for being excellent layers, and they can actually outperform chickens in this department. With ducks, you can have a steady supply of eggs, which are delicious and larger than chicken eggs. It's a rewarding experience that can add a unique touch to your breakfast table.

Interestingly, ducks were once poised to take the lead as the primary egg providers. However, chickens gained popularity due to their adaptability to intensive farming methods. Despite this turn, ducks remain a fantastic option for small-scale egg production, especially if you're looking for a more diverse egg selection.

Beyond the realm of eggs, ducks offer some unique advantages over chickens. One of these benefits is their natural talent for pest control. They are excellent at foraging and can keep pests in check. Unlike chickens, they won't scratch up the ground and create a mess, making them a valuable addition to your garden maintenance team. They are the low-maintenance pets of the poultry world. They're great at scavenging through the veggie patch and doing a solid job of hunting down those slimy slugs and other critters.

Caring for ducks is surprisingly straightforward, too, making it even more appealing for both beginners and experienced farmers. While a pond can be a wonderful addition to your farm, it's not an absolute requirement for raising ducks. They're content with smaller water sources, such as a kiddie pool or shallow container. This adaptability adds to their charm and makes them relatively easy to incorporate into your farm setup.

Before diving into the duck-keeping world, you should take a few practical steps. Check with your local authorities to ensure that ducks are allowed in your area. Most places are perfectly fine with a small number of ducks, but it's always a good idea to ensure you follow the rules. If you have neighbors nearby, it's also a courteous gesture to have a friendly chat with them about your plans.

Chapter 1: The Benefits of Raising Ducks

Ducks are not the first animals that come to mind when people think about raising livestock. People typically imagine raising chickens, pigs, or cows. You usually get asked if you are a dog or a cat person, never a duck person. The extent to which society interacts with ducks is limited to prints on children's pajamas, Disney cartoons, and occasionally feeding them at your local park. Aside from being ridiculously cute, these overlooked birds can be a wonderful addition to a family or homestead.

Aside from being ridiculously cute, ducks can be a wonderful addition to a family or homestead.

Ducks come in many varieties and can be raised for several reasons, including meat, egg, and fertilizer production. Furthermore, these highly intelligent birds make great companions. Some therapists have recommended ducks as emotional support animals because they can connect with people. Humans have had a long relationship with domesticated ducks that has spanned over 500 years. For that reason alone, you will not have any problems researching what is best for the birds.

Ducks have a unique, graceful serenity that can be awe-inspiring. They are similar to dogs in that they can form meaningful attachments. One of the most common phenomena recorded among duck species when it comes to bonding is the imprinting that ducklings do at birth. If you are the first living being that a duck sees moving after it hatches, it will imprint on you and follow you around as if you were its mother. As fellow social organisms, humans share a kinship with ducks that leads to an interspecies understanding.

Ducks provide meat and eggs and can be a huge benefit to a farm ecosystem. Wandering ducks eat insects, snails, and weeds. They can then be used as part of a permaculture system that limits the use of pesticides. By minimizing pesticides in farming, ducks can help farmers transition to cleaner ways of producing food by decreasing soil and water contamination. In addition to pest control, ducks can produce natural fertilizer and compost.

Opening yourself up to the unfolding possibility of a beneficial co-existence with ducks introduces you to a new, fulfilling world. Once you learn the basics and can execute key principles of duck raising, the rewards will become increasingly apparent. Taking this leap can be one of the most enlightening decisions you ever make. Moreover, ducks are relatively low-maintenance, so you will not break your back to care for them. Low effort, coupled with innumerable benefits, is a favorable route worth exploring if you're thinking of getting a new animal.

The Pleasure of Raising Ducks

One of the stand-out aspects of raising ducks is the pleasure it can bring. Imagine the old man reading his newspaper in the park, leisurely throwing pieces of bread at passing ducks. Doesn't that image bring immediate relaxation? There's something truly grounding about interacting with ducks. The peace of mind that comes from connecting with ducks is indescribable. You will not fully understand that until you experience the miracle of raising a duck from when it was a fluffy, yellow duckling to full adulthood. The social nature of ducks allows them to form deep bonds, which are quite fulfilling for humans who share a similar drive to maintain relationships.

Ducks are beautiful to look at. These gorgeous birds come in all shapes, sizes, and colors. Sitting back and absorbing their majesty facilitates a deep sense of gratitude for the natural world. There is nothing like watching a trail of ducklings follow their mother on a pond. The way they glide on top of the water is splendidly satisfying. Ducks just seem to have an unexplainably inviting aura that you can't help but want to be around, especially when you start interacting with them regularly. You cannot fully understand what it means to raise ducks until you share a space with them.

The peace of mind that comes from connecting with ducks is indescribable.
https://unsplash.com/photos/JDzoTGfoogA

If you are raising ducks for eggs and meat, the feeling of raising your produce from birth is magical. Eating your own food is worlds apart from buying plastic-wrapped food in the grocery store. There is something primal about tapping into the ancient tradition of raising domesticated animals. It is as if your ancestral memory is activated, linking you with the long lineage of people who used agriculture to propel civilization forward. As humanity moves into the next age of agriculture, where environmental concerns are taking center stage, raising ducks seems to be a way forward for conscious poultry production.

There are also financial benefits to raising ducks for eggs and meat. The duck market continues to grow, and there is room for more expansion, with turkey and chicken farming still being far ahead of duck farming. This relatively untapped market, compared to other poultry meats, has the potential to explode, especially considering the wide variety of environments in which ducks can thrive and their resilience. The satisfaction of profit can be a motivating factor to begin your duck-raising operation.

Egg and Meat Production

A primary benefit of raising ducks is the meat and eggs you can harvest. Chicken eggs are eaten in almost every household, but duck eggs are just as delicious. The beauty of ducks is that they are species that can exponentially outlay chickens. It is baffling that more farms have not embraced ducks for egg production. They do not lay daily, but you can get over 300 eggs from one duck over a year. A few ducks can completely eradicate the need for you to buy eggs from a supermarket. You'll also be able to sell the surplus. Ducks can be raised alongside chickens, so you do not have to abandon the idea of chicken farming altogether. You can introduce variety into your egg consumption by combining ducks and chickens.

Generally, ducks are healthier than chickens, so you'll have fewer disease-related issues. Ducks are also more equipped to survive in the winter due to their fat layers and thick feathers. Some species can even sleep outside in the rain and the snow. Surprisingly, ducks can even deal with hot weather better than chickens. Although chickens and ducks are both noisy, ducks tend to be quieter throughout the day. Even though they can be loud, their quacking is not consistent.

Most people consume chicken eggs, but duck eggs are better in many ways. The higher fat content in duck eggs makes for a richer flavor. Duck eggs are larger as well, so you do not only get more in terms of number, but you get greater size quantity as well. Many pastry chefs prefer duck eggs because their high-fat content can be better for baking recipes. Therefore, the superiority of duck eggs should propel you to embrace this nutritious source of protein. The noticeable switch from chicken eggs to duck eggs will have you wondering why you didn't start raising ducks ages ago.

Duck meat is a lean source of protein. Considering the obesity issues that the Western world suffers from, switching from red meat to duck meat can be life-saving. In addition to protein, duck meat is also a brilliant source of iron. Eating a serving of duck meat can provide you with half the daily iron intake. The nutrient-rich meat also contains B vitamins, which help maintain healthy hair, skin, and muscles. Duck meat has a lower fat content than chicken, so it can be useful for health-conscious people and gym-goers.

Nearly every part of the duck is edible, and the parts that can't be eaten are still useful, like the feathers or offal. Therefore, if you raise ducks for produce, nothing will go to waste. People dine on all kinds of duck meat, including the liver and gizzards. Duck liver is considered a delicacy in many parts of the world due to its unique fattiness. Their meat can be eaten with rice and vegetables for a hearty, wholesome meal. It can be prepared in various ways, including barbeque, roasting, or even in a stew.

Duck meat has more vitamins and minerals and lower cholesterol amounts than chicken, making it a healthier option. Many parts of the world have a crisis in obesity and food-related diseases like diabetes and hypertension. Exploring duck farming could be one of the solutions to addressing some of the world's nutrition issues. If duck farming is more widely embraced, the price of healthier meat will be driven down. Moreover, the larger size means that people will get more meat for their buck.

Pest Control

If you are growing produce, ducks can be a good deterrent to various kinds of pests. Seeing how they spend a significant portion of their day foraging, ducks love feeding on bugs and snails. People who raise ducks usually save a lot of money on pesticides. Even though they're very effective, pesticides, over time, can negatively impact your soil because they destroy micro-diversity that provides essential nutrients to plants. Using ducks as a form of pest control can keep your soil alive.

Asian farmers have traditionally used ducks to control the insect population in rice paddies. Species like the Indian runner have been bred to have longer limbs to cover more ground. Using your ducks for pest control can create a robust ecosystem on a large farm, smallholding, and backyard. Since they naturally forage with little intervention, ducks can basically become your partners in tending the field. With pest control ducks, your birds happily feed on insects, your plants are protected, and you'll enjoy a high-quality, organic harvest.

Ducks can be a good deterrent to various kinds of pests.
https://www.pexels.com/photo/ducklings-eating-on-ground-12295250/

Considering that climate change is propelling the globe into a new way of functioning, incorporating animals for cleaner farming methods may be necessary. The minimal harm that ducks cause and their relatively low cost of maintenance may make the bird a logical solution for embracing environmentally friendly practices in food production. Ducks can be bred for meat, which can be a useful alternative to breeding cows that generate excessive methane gas. Introducing ducks into your homestead can build a mutually beneficial ecosystem that can maintain a healthy, natural balance.

Ducks do not exclusively help with insect pests but can extend their services to include weed eradication. Ducks are both foragers and grazers. They eat weeds and small plants. If they are allowed to independently forage in your field, that will reduce the cost of their feed. The combination of weeds and insects will be a great supplement for your duck's diet. Common weed species like dandelion greens are a favorite snack for many breeds. Unlike chickens, ducks are less damaging to your plants because they eat taller shrubs and do not dig the ground up.

Small snakes, mice, and frogs are also not safe when ducks are around. These pests can wreak havoc on your crops. The hunting prowess of ducks can help maintain a low mouse population, which can contribute to avoiding infestations. Mice dig your crops out at the roots so they can threaten an entire harvest. Poisoning mice can lead to the soil getting damaged and may result in other wildlife you did not plan to kill being affected. If you have children on your property, using poison can be a catastrophic hazard. Children are curious and spend a lot of time playing outside, which means they could easily come into harmful contact with poison being used in a homestead. Using ducks for pest control can help you craft a safer environment for young ones visiting or living with you.

The Resilience of Ducks

Some cultures use ducks as a symbol of stability. This makes perfect sense when considering ducks are some of the most resilient animals. Of all the domestic poultry humans raise, ducks are the least susceptible to disease and have spectacular immunity. Therefore, whether you raise ducks for meat, eggs, or as companions, you can rest assured that they will not easily fall ill. Their strong immunities and resilience to extreme temperatures make them one of the most low-maintenance animals to keep.

In their natural environment, ducks face all kinds of external threats, including predators and the challenges of living in robust habitats. They have evolved to be strong and intelligent. Some duck species migrate over long distances and can spend extended stretches of time in the air. Furthermore, ducks are social creatures who often fight during mating seasons. The combination of duck behavior and psychology grouped with the tough environments they come from has created a lovingly resilient creature that takes no nonsense.

Ducks are an amazing starting point if you plan on catering to a diverse farm, whether for subsistence or commercial. They can be used to introduce you to the world of farming without overwhelming you because of how resilient they are. Instead of picking high-maintenance animals as your initial investment, you can begin with ducks that can provide high-end eggs and premium meat.

Ducks are not prone to diseases, so they are safe animals to keep around people and livestock. Moreover, the temperature control that makes ducks adapt to changing weather conditions makes them a brilliant option in the wake of global warming. Where many animals will perish due to the changing climate, ducks may be the best poultry option to explore to adapt to climate change. The sustainability that ducks present by laying large eggs and providing a lot of meat while playing a crucial role in the ecosystem as a predator and fertilizer makes ducks one of the most environmentally friendly livestock. Unlike cows, which take up a lot of space and produce greenhouse gases, and chickens, which often require all types of medication because they are sickly, ducks can be the sustainable meat of the future.

Duck Fertilizer and Regenerative Farming

With a mounting environmental crisis largely contributed to the livestock farming industry, ducks can present a way to embrace more environmentally friendly farming methods. Essentially, ducks are the perfect animal to create a permaculture environment with. Permaculture farming is an eco-friendly way of approaching agriculture where you construct regenerative ecosystems that work with the local fauna and flora. Pest control ducks already present a powerful permaculture asset but also provide fertilizer.

Duck waste is nitrogen-rich, giving your soil much-needed nutrients to replenish it with each harvest. Macro-nutrient nitrogen is crucial for plants to develop amino acids, the building blocks of protein that contribute to growth. Therefore, nitrogen will help your plants grow faster and bigger. Many farmers use artificial nitrogen fertilizers, which are well-formulated to help plants grow. However, these artificial fertilizers tend to focus on providing the plants with nutrients instead of replenishing the soil. Using a natural nitrogen fertilizer like duck waste is superior in the long term.

The best environment for ducks is a swampy marsh with a pond or another water source. With the ducks spending a lot of time in the water, the runoff can be built into an irrigation system with fertilizer combined with the water. A duck pond can help you save on your water bill and can be a more sustainable method of irrigating a farm. A water source with ducks creates a living system that beneficially contributes to the biodiversity of your land.

Poultry meat has also been used as a way to fertilize the soil. In many parts of the Western world, offal from poultry is not consumed or made into processed meat like nuggets or sausages. In a homestead setup, a creative way to use the offal is to bury it underneath the soil and plant on top of it. This can be used as a way to restore nutrients to the soil. Inedible parts of the duck can be used in this fertilizing process, such as its bill and feet.

Many duck breeds can be aggressive and bite people when threatened. However, some breeds are very docile. These calmer breeds are perfect as pets, especially around kids. Ducks are intelligent birds that can be taught tricks and commands. As pets, they can be trained to embrace cuddles and form a strong bond as a member of the family. Keeping one as a pet allows you to still get the benefits of fertilizer and pest control without having to slaughter the animal if you are uncomfortable with that. Whether you are a vegan or a meat-eater, ducks can be the perfect addition to your farm, yard, or smallholding.

Welcome to the World of Raising Ducks

By exploring the benefits of raising ducks, you have taken a significant step forward to uncover the layers of contentment buried underneath duck farming. As you raise your ducks from chicks to adulthood and notice their evolution, you won't be able to help but feel a certain sense of kinship with the animal. Ducks are social, intelligent, and emotional, so they are easy to establish a close relationship with. Their robust personalities and cuteness will definitely tug at your heartstrings and leave you with endless stories.

Ducks are social, intelligent, and emotional, so they are easy to establish a close relationship with.
https://www.pexels.com/photo/children-sitting-on-a-picnic-blanket-10652690/

The beauty of duck raising is in the process of having patience until your inevitable reward. The meat, eggs, or companionship you gain will prevent cognitive dissonance if you take the informed path to raising ducks. Embracing an environmentally conscious and cruelty-free method of raising ducks can present a guilt-free emotional, financial, and social fulfillment endeavor. If you are still questioning whether you should raise ducks when you have the space and time, the answer is to go for it! Ducks may be the best option for a lovable pet and livestock when you weigh the pros and cons of raising different animals. Their low-maintenance resilience makes them an awesome project to explore as an entry point into raising animals. Furthermore, their novelty and beauty will keep you entertained and wrapped around their cute little webbed feet. There has never been a better time to start raising ducks than right now, so continue reading and prepare to start this rewarding journey.

Chapter 2: Understanding Duck Behaviors

If you owned a pet before, you know how important it is to build a relationship with them. Every strong relationship requires healthy communication. Animals, however, don't communicate in the same way humans do. Due to their underdeveloped cognitive abilities and intellect, along with their less-evolved vocal cords, animals cannot speak like humans, and they never will be able to, at least not in the near future. That doesn't mean they cannot communicate, though.

Most dog owners have learned to relate different types of barks to different moods. For instance, did you know that a high-pitched whine often indicates anxiety? In cats, the kind of "meow" you hear most often (moderate pitch, medium-long cry) generally means that they want something.

Vocal communication isn't the only way to understand animals. Their behavior and actions can often be interpreted as something comprehensible. For example, you may have noticed that a cow usually lets its tail hang freely. That almost always means they feel safe. When it is stiff and tucked between its legs, it can indicate they are sick or anxious.

Do ducks, on the other hand, display communicative behavior? The good news is, they do! While you obviously won't be able to converse with them, you can certainly understand their sounds, differentiate between various noises, and comprehend their social structure to better interpret their behavior.

Duck Communication

Ducks primarily communicate vocally. Sometimes, they also use body language to express what they want. If you can pick up on their behavioral cues, you'll be well on your way to building a good rapport with them.

Vocal Communication and Unique Sounds

The most common sound a duck makes, something you had learned in elementary school, is "quack." Dogs bark, cats meow, and ducks quack. Do you know that different types of quacks mean different things? Apart from the basic quack, ducks also make a wide range of sounds, from a meek squeak to a formidable bark. As a general rule, the louder the sound, the more pressing the message.

Ducks primarily communicate vocally.
© *Marie-Lan Nguyen, CC BY 2.5 DEED* <*https://creativecommons.org/licenses/by/2.5/*>
Wikimedia Commons:
https://commons.wikimedia.org/wiki/File:Anas_platyrhynchos_quacking_Jardin_des_Plantes_Par is_2013-04-22.jpg

- **Quack:** Whenever you hear the loud quack sound, you can generally deduce that there are ducks nearby. Not all ducks, however, produce that sound. Only the females (hens) in Mallard ducks can generate that quintessential sound.

  Additionally, not all quacks mean the same thing. The most common interpretation of a loud quack is a mother duck calling out to its ducklings. It may also be a call for its male partner (drake) to mate. When you hear a single duck quacking in a raft of ducks, it is probably claiming a drake as its own.

Nocturnal ducks usually don't make a lot of noise. Since ducks are primarily diurnal, the nocturnal ones understand they should not disturb most of their sleeping flock with needless noise. So, when they do quack at night, it's generally a warning sign that a predator is nearby.

If pet ducks are quacking a lot around you, it may mean that they are excited to see you and eager to play with you. Don't jump into their space just yet, though. Check if they are about to lay eggs because they also tend to quack a lot.

- **Honk:** This is another frequently heard sound among ducks. Again, it is more common among the hens in many breeds. It ordinarily implies that it is trying to make its position known to its partner, especially if they are far apart in an unknown terrain (not when they are in a large crowd of ducks).

  Honking while in a flock of ducks may mean the same thing as quacking - they have selected their partner. It may also mean that they have detected a predator in the vicinity (regardless of the time of day or night).

- **Hiss:** The hisses of ducks aren't normally as continuous as a snake's. They are more low-pitched and grainy, with quite a few halts in between. Both males and females of many species are known to produce this sound, especially when they are afraid of something. It's more of a whispered conversation, an apprehensive murmur, the same way you may communicate with your friends when you are threatened to stay quiet by someone.

- **Purr:** Like cats, ducks also purr, often for the same reason. Your pet duck may start purring while you are petting them, implying that they like it and want you to continue doing it.

- **Growl:** Just as your stomach growls when you're hungry, ducks growl when they want food. It's more of a low-pitch apprehensive growl than the dangerous bark of a dog. Keep a bowl of oats or birdseed ready when they make this sound.

Other unique sounds that ducks make are whistling, groaning, squeaking, croaking, sighing, and even hooting like an owl! But these are less commonly heard among domesticated ducks.

Body Language and Behavioral Cues

While sounds may be the most important form of communication with your ducks, understanding their body language comes in at a close second. They look amazingly cute when they blow bubbles in the pond, but is there a deeper meaning to the act? What do all their small behavioral cues mean, like head tilting at odd times?

- **Walking One behind the Other:** You may have noticed this often. Whenever a family of ducks walks on land, they waddle in a straight line, one behind the other. Unlike humans and many other animals, they don't usually walk side by side. In ducks, this behavior shows that they trust each other. The one leading the flock guides the rest on their way by looking straight ahead. The ducks behind the leader tend to look anywhere but the front to ensure their group isn't surprised from the sides or back.

- **Sleeping with an Open Eye:** If you own a couple of ducks and a few ducklings, you may have noticed that the adults often sleep with one eye open. They are actually asleep, but half their brain is alert with their single open eye, keeping a watch for predators.

Ducks watch out for predators while sleeping with an eye open.
https://www.pexels.com/photo/close-up-photography-of-ducks-1024501/

- **Blowing Bubbles**: You may find it adorable when your ducks blow bubbles in the pond. They aren't exactly having fun but are removing any dirt or debris stuck in their nostrils.

- **Staring with Head Tilted**: Are your ducks giving you a thousand-yard stare with their head tilted to one side? Don't worry, they aren't scared. They are watching through their peripheral vision for either predators or food.

- **Wagging Their Tail Feathers**: Just like a dog shows excitement or happiness by wagging its tail, ducks show these emotions the same way. If they wag their tail feathers when you approach, it means they are happy to see you. On the other hand, they may simply have emerged from the pond and are drying themselves off. If that's the case, you may also find them preening the feathers on the rest of their body, distributing essential oils evenly throughout.

- **Digging Holes in Mud Puddles**: This is one of the ways in which ducks put their long beaks to good use. They have learned from experience that mud puddles usually have bugs and other insects beneath the bottom surface. They are simply foraging for food.

The Act of Imprinting

Did you know that you can make ducklings trust you without doing anything? Soon after a duckling hatches, it will learn to trust the one whom it sees the most. This process is called imprinting. It may take a few months or even years for human infants to imprint on their mothers. A duckling is quick to trust, imprinting on its mother or fellow ducklings (whoever it sees the most) as fast as within an hour!

You'll also be delighted to know that ducklings can imprint on you! Place the eggs in an incubator and wait for them to hatch. As soon as they crack open and the duckling peeks out, ensure that the first thing it sees is your face. Stay with it for an hour or two, and let it keep seeing you. Pet, caress, or handle it, and even talk to it if you can.

A duckling is quick to trust, imprinting on its mother or fellow ducklings (whoever it sees the most) as fast as within an hour!

You won't know right away if the duckling has imprinted on you. When it grows up and starts exhibiting any of the excitement behaviors mentioned above when you approach (like wagging its tail feathers), then you can be somewhat certain that you succeeded. Does the duck let you easily handle and care for it when it's sick? Only then can you be absolutely sure that it trusts you!

Social Structure of Duck Flocks

Ducks have a social structure in their flocks. It helps them reduce internal conflicts and live in harmony with each other. Even if they do reach a conflict, the flock leader ensures that it is resolved or that a compromise is reached.

Social Hierarchy

The social hierarchy or pecking order in ducks is loosely based on physical appearance. The stronger the duck appears to be, the higher it will be placed. Age doesn't really factor in. A duckling who has just matured into a healthy duck with graceful features may start leading a pack of other, more experienced ducks.

A pecking order is more commonly observed in hens. Did you know that a flock leader always lays its eggs first? The other ducks have to hold until the hens higher on the social ladder have dropped their eggs in the nest. Sometimes, a better-organized flock may stand on each other with the leader at the top and lay their eggs one by one (top first). That way, if a predator is lurking around, they can protect their eggs together. Also, it may be the lead hen's way to stress its leadership.

Drakes also have a social hierarchy, which can be observed when they are mating. If you have several drakes but just one hen, you may have noticed that the ducks mate individually. The first drake to mate is usually the strongest one and the leader of the flock.

Ducks have a pecking order while eating, too. The next time that you leave a bowl of feed near their nesting area, wait a while and observe them eat. They will rarely ever huddle around the bowl together. The first few ducks that come to feed will be the leaders of the flock, followed by the next in the hierarchy.

If you observe them every day, you will notice that the last (lowest order) batch of ducks never goes hungry. That is because ducks can assess the quantity of feed very well and distribute it evenly among the entire flock.

Flirting and Mating

It's a joy to watch ducks flirt with each other. You may even learn a thing or two! The courting habits of ducks are no different to humans. Have you noticed drakes emerge from the water, dripping wet, flaunting their plush-soaked feathers by ruffling them in the sun? How often have you seen men do the same thing after emerging from a public pool, ruffling their hair while flaunting their bodies?

The hens usually nod their heads in approval. When they also flatten themselves, belly down, in the water, it is an invitation for the drake to mount her. If the female doesn't approve of the male, the latter may have a few other flirting techniques, like scooping up water in its beak and flipping it at the hen.

Ducks are able to mate in the water as well as on land. They feel more comfortable in the water because the buoyancy lets the hen spread herself more freely. Granted, the water's instability may make them lose their balance while mounting, but the drake holds on to the neck of the hen with its beak to avoid falling off.

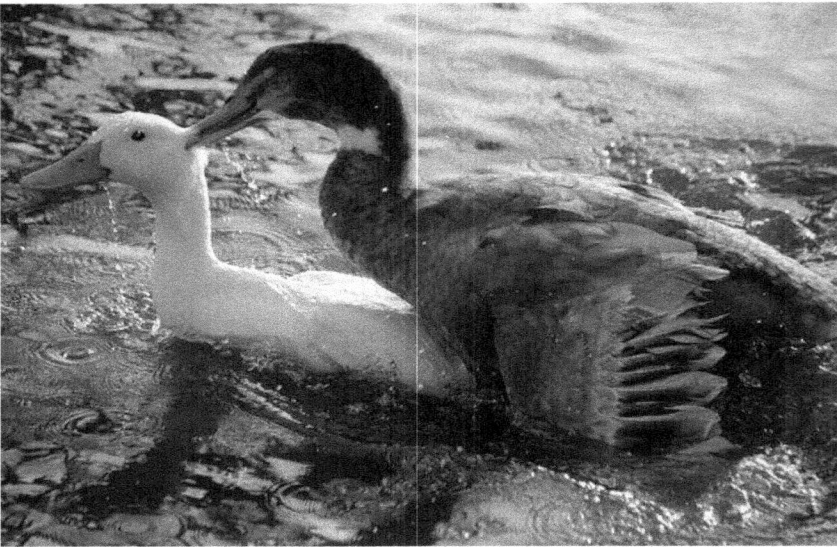

Ducks are able to mate in the water as well as on land.
https://pixabay.com/photos/ducks-birds-animals-mating-6384735/

The act of mating itself is not as graceful as you would think it to be. The uninitiated may feel like your ducks are fighting, with the drake trying to pin down the hen. At times, multiple drakes may converge on a single hen, and neither of them gets hurt in the process. It's just how their mating ritual is. They aren't monogamous.

The males are the most amorous of the lot. A drake will have one female, which it prizes above others. It will feed, care for, and even spend the most time with her. That won't hold it back from mating with other nearby hens. The drakes are like the kings and emperors of yore, who married the queen of their heart but also kept several mistresses.

On the other hand, a female duck has only one male romantic interest at a time (it may have several in its lifetime). However, other drakes are free to mate with it if they want, even if the hen has no desire for them. Consent doesn't really feature in their relationship, but don't feel too bad. That's the way they live.

Common Behavioral Problems and Their Solutions

Ducks are living, breathing beings with health and behavioral issues like any other animal. Due to their relatively advanced intelligence and high emotional quotient, they also tend to face psychological problems. They usually don't keep things bottled up inside. Their problems are often reflected in their behavior. The most common ones include,

Weird Vocals

Is your waterfowl making a weird sound? Try to relate it to any of the vocals mentioned in the "Duck Communication" section. If it's neither the fairly common honk nor the immensely rare hoot, the duck may be trying to express a problem in its health, like an infection. Is the sound low-pitched or hoarse? It may be trying to alert the presence of a predator. Either way, you need to take it to a veterinarian to ensure it doesn't spread to the other ducks if it's an infection.

Low Egg Frequency or Quality

Does your mother duck rarely lay any eggs (say, no more than once or twice a week)? Regardless of the frequency, are the eggs laid of poor quality (look rotten or bad)? It is a common problem during winter, which can be easily avoided by increasing the amount of their food. Ducks tend to spend more energy in the cold weather to keep their body temperature in check. Hence, they need more food in especially harsh winters to keep their energy levels up.

Overeating

Humans tend to overeat during stressful times. Ducks, on the other hand, may overeat because of humans. It really depends on the diet you are giving them. If you are including a lot of bread and junk food in their diet, it may cause several health issues. Stick with grains or oats. If you don't have them stocked, let them forage for themselves for a while. Their health problems may just vanish into thin air. If they persist, visit a vet.

Causing Self-Harm

Does your fowl often pick its feathers? Does it scratch itself to the point of bloodying its skin? Does it tend to cause harm to itself in any way? They are displaying antisocial behavior due to increased stress. Are you keeping the duck isolated from its family? Do you own just one duck? Ducks are social animals by nature, and when they don't get a chance to interact with their fellow ducks or ducklings, they may start to harm themselves. Unite it with its family or bring new ducks into the fold.

If the duck inflicts self-harm while present in a group, it may be infected with a parasite. Take it to a vet right away.

Repetitive Actions

Is your duck exhibiting repetitive behavior, like waddling back and forth or circling in the same small area? This is another indication of stress. It may be due to isolation from the flock. Alternatively, are your ducks confined in a congested space? They are used to, or have evolved to, live free and unhindered in the wild. They need a lot of space to ensure the stability of their mental health.

Let them roam around in your backyard from time to time. Ducks are called waterfowl for a reason. If you don't have a private pool or pond, lead them to a pool in the neighborhood (provided the owner agrees to let the ducks jump in!) Lack of sexual activity could also be a major cause of stress, so ensure each drake has a hen to mate with.

Chapter 3: Choosing the Right Breed of Duck

Ducks make fantastic additions to your farm and can thrive independently and alongside chickens. If you've ever raised poultry before, you're likely aware of the joy it brings, and raising ducks offers an equally rewarding experience. Ducks take pleasure in exploring the farm or yard, much like chickens, and they share the appetite for feasting on insects, including larger ones like slugs and grasshoppers, which sets them apart from their feathered counterparts.

The world of ducks boasts a diverse array of breeds, and for those new to duck-keeping, selecting the right breed can seem daunting. In this chapter, we aim to simplify the process by providing you with insights into various duck breeds. We'll delve into their distinctive characteristics, specific requirements, and the unique contributions they bring to your farm. Furthermore, we'll delve into the strengths and weaknesses of each breed, including their temperament, egg production capabilities, size, foraging prowess, and adaptability to varying climatic conditions. This comprehensive guide will equip you with the knowledge you need to make informed decisions when it comes to choosing and caring for your ducks.

The Various Duck Breeds

Finding the ideal duck breed begins with a clear understanding of your specific goals and needs. Your choice of duck breed should align with the purpose you have in mind. Here are some crucial questions to guide your decision-making:

1. **Determine Your Purpose**: What role do you envision for your ducks?

   - Are you primarily interested in egg production?

   - Do you seek a duck breed renowned for its meat yield?

   - Are you in search of charming backyard companions capable of pest control?

   - Are you interested in ducks known for their foraging skills, sociable nature, or calm demeanor?

   - Is heritage breed conservation a priority, leading you to consider breeds classified as threatened or critical?

2. **Consider Additional Factors**: Beyond your primary purpose, think about other factors that matter to you:

   - **Size**: Larger breeds may offer better protection against aerial predators.

   - **Aesthetic Appeal**: Are you looking for visually striking duck breeds?

   - **Mothering Ability**: If breeding is part of your plan, consider a breed that excels in nurturing ducklings.

3. **Assess Your Commitment**: Recognize the level of effort you're willing to invest in your chosen duck breed's care and maintenance:

   - Are you prepared to gather eggs regularly?

   - Can you handle the needs of larger breeds, including assisting with hatching if necessary?

   - If you prefer chatty ducks, are you ready for continuous communication with them?

Once you've determined what you can offer and your primary objectives, you'll be better equipped to identify the most suitable duck breed for your farm or lifestyle. Keep in mind that the best breed for you is the one that aligns with your specific requirements.

Top Duck Breeds
Indian Runner

The Indian Runner boasts one of the most unique builds in the duck world. It is an unusual-looking breed of domestic duck.

The Indian Runner boasts one of the most unique builds in the duck world.
Bjoern Clauss, CC BY-SA 2.5 <https://creativecommons.org/licenses/by-sa/2.5>, via Wikimedia Commons: https://commons.wikimedia.org/wiki/File:Runner-ducks.jpg

Characteristics

They belong to the lightweight category of domestic duck breed. They have long necks, slender heads, and slim bodies. Their long neck has earned them the description of a "wine bottle." Due to their longer neck, their eyes are set high, with a straight bill. Their legs are positioned way behind the back of their body, which is different from other duck breeds. An Indian Runner can run and at the same time shuffle quickly due to the position of their legs and the shape of their bodies.

When agitated, they stand fully erect. Normally, they have a 45 - 75% degree of carriage above eye view. From the crown of their head to their tail tip, the small female's height is 20 to 26 inches, while the taller male's height is about 70 inches.

The drake's tail tip is a bit curled, while that of the ducks is flat. You might be unable to tell the difference between the drakes and the duck until both mature.

When compared to other breeds, they have 14 color varieties, including Trout and white, Fawn, Mallard, Silver, Apricot Dusky, Chocolate, Cumberland Blue, Black, Apricot Trout, Blue, Blue Trout, Blue Dusky, Light brown, Dark brown. Eight varieties of runners are registered with the American Standard of Perfection, and they include gray, Cumberland blue, chocolate, buff, black, penciled, white, and the original Fawn and white.

The ducks have a body weight averaging 1.4 to 2kg, while the drake's body weight is averaging 1.6 to 2.3 kg.

Needs

Indian Runners don't need special dietary or living quarters. They only need a conducive space with a sleeping spot, clean water, clean bedding, and regular poultry bird food to keep them happy and healthy. Unlike other duck breeds, Indian Runners require less water. A water tub to dunk their head into is enough.

Unique Value

Indian Runners are wonderful foragers and major egg producers. They are also good for controlling pests.

Temperament

Indian Runners are docile and friendly. They get along well with other pets like dogs and cats. However, they become very aggressive while protecting their little ones or when they sense danger and feel threatened.

Egg Production

Indian runners are well-known for their ability to lay eggs. They lay over 300 to 350 eggs yearly. At the least, they lay 5 to 6 eggs a week. The eggs Indian Runners lay are large and pastel green in color. They are sought after due to their distinct flavor, making them excellent for baking.

Foraging Ability

Indian Runners are popular independent foragers who enjoy hunting for hidden snacks like insects, snails, slugs, and seeds.

Adaptability

They can adapt to all climates, even those extremely hot or cold. Their egg production might reduce during cold weather, but it will not cease. No matter the hardiness of the ducks, precautions should be taken during the harsh climate to ensure they have access to clean water and shade. Their coop should be properly ventilated at all times, too.

Khaki Campbell

If you are looking for a beginner-friendly duck capable of laying more eggs, then Khaki Campbell is your go-to duck. Khaki Campbell originated from England and was introduced to the world around 1898. Mrs. Adele Campbell of Uley, Gloucestershire, England, developed the Khaki Campbell ducks. Being a poultry keeper, she purchased an Indian Runner, which she crossbred with the Rouen and other wild ducks, resulting in khaki Campbell.

If you are looking for a beginner-friendly duck capable of laying more eggs, then Khaki Campbell is your go-to duck.

Keith, CC BY 2.0 <https://creativecommons.org/licenses/by/2.0>, via Wikimedia Commons: https://commons.wikimedia.org/wiki/File:Khaki_Campbell_female.jpg

Characteristics

Mistaking a typical Mallard duck for a Khaki Campbell duck is very easy. A Khaki Campbell has a long neck with a boat-shaped body. Its feathers and wings have a light or dark khaki color. Depending on the duck's gender, a Khaki Campbell duck can have a black or green bill with dark orange to brown legs. The female Khaki Campbell ducks often have dark features like khaki feathers, while the male counterparts have light features like light khaki wings and feathers.

On a Khaki Campbell, you will notice curls of white on the duck's chest. These ducks have beautiful feathers, and the color range of their skin is from white to a bit yellow, based on the types of feed given to them. Khaki Campbell ducks are known to be medium-sized ducks, with their weights never exceeding 4.5 lbs. for both the males and the females.

The female average weight is from 3.5 to 4 lbs., while the male average is from 4 to 4.5 lbs. In height, both are averaging from 1.5 to 2 feet.

Needs

Khaki Campbell ducks do not require a special diet. As ducklings, you can feed them non-medicinal chick starter feeds. Once they are 3 months old, you can feed them game birds, chicken feed, or waterfowl. Due to a potential choking hazard risk, scratch-style feed is not recommended for ducks. Nevertheless, pellet varieties of chicken feed and crumble are known for feeding domestic breeds of ducks. If the Khaki Campbell duck is in a coop or duck house, endeavor to feed them grit to enable them to properly digest their food without any issues.

Unique Value

Most people raise Khaki Campbell ducks mainly for their egg-laying ability. It is a breed that fits duck commercial farming based on its popularity as one of the best egg-laying ducks. This breed is also used for meat production. They are exceptional foragers and would eat anything from various invertebrate pests they encounter. They are your backyard and garden rangers who would take care of anything that might sting or cause itching to your family or threaten your crops.

Temperament

The Khaki Campbell ducks are strong, robust, and active. They are calm, friendly, and passive when raised by hands until maturity, irrespective of the misconception of them being skittish or of flighty behavior.

Egg Production

This duck's area of strength is that it can lay up to 300 eggs per year, 4 to 6 medium-sized white eggs per week. It is highly regarded for its dual purpose because of its ability to produce both eggs and meat. They start laying eggs as early as 21 weeks old.

Foraging Ability

This breed has excellent foraging ability and should be given room to roam. They don't do well when confined.

Adaptability

Khaki Campbell ducks can survive in every climate due to their cold, hardy nature.

Pekin Ducks

Although old, American Pekins is a well-known dual-purpose duck known for its meat and egg production. This breed is now in many countries and is one of the most known breeds for commercial purposes. The main reason it's called American Pekin is to differentiate it from the German Pekin.

American Pekins is a well-known dual-purpose duck known for its meat and egg production.

Characteristics

The American Pekin duck is beautiful to behold. They have long necks and bodies, yellow skin, and large breasts. The color of their feathers is either creamy white or white. Their bill is yellow, and their legs are orange-yellow or reddish. Their rump is overturned, and their posture is more vertical than dabbing ducks. When you closely observe these ducks, you'll see their eyes are grayish-blue colored irises. The weight of a Pekin duck is from 8 to 12 pounds.

Needs

Pekins need a clean space to shield them from rain and wind, a fence to keep them contained, and access to water and food. Due to its limited flight ability, the fence should be low. Pekins enjoy both natural and commercial food. If you give them free-range access, they can eat their favorite food from nature. In commercial production farming, commercial feed is usually fed to these ducks. The ducklings can be fed with chick starter feed.

Unique Value

Perkins performs dual-purpose functions. They are raised for meat production in America. The duck meat consumed in the United States is 95% Perkins duck. This breed is also perfect for egg production. It can give you an average of 200 white-colored eggs yearly.

Temperament

Perkins ducks are intelligent, non-aggressive, and friendly. Those who raise them either as pets or egg birds can pet them from time to time. Pekins like to be touched. You can lay them upside down in your lap and stroke their bellies.

Egg Production

Pekins can average 200 to 300 large eggs yearly. When a Pekin hen is 5 to 6 months old, she begins to lay eggs.

Meat Production

This is the primary reason Pekin ducks are reared in America. 95% of the duck meat consumed by the average American is Perkin duck meat. The meat is rich in protein and has a tasty flavor. It doesn't have the texture or greasy taste of other duck meat. At 6 weeks old, a Pekin, weighing around 6 pounds, is ready to be butchered. A Jumbo Pekin's average weight is around 9 to 11 pounds when they reach 12 weeks old. The increased weight associated with Pekin ducks is one of the main reasons they are reared for their meat.

Foraging Ability

They're excellent foragers as they can forage for most of their diet.

Adaptability

Due to its hardy nature and strong and resilient immune system, Pekin ducks can adjust to any climate.

Muscovy Ducks

The Muscovy duck is a well-known big domestic duck breed that originated in North America and is found in states like Massachusetts, Florida, and Hawaii. This is the only domesticated breed not obtained from the Mallard duck.

The Muscovy duck is a well-known big domestic duck breed.
Fredricx, CC BY-SA 4.0 <https://creativecommons.org/licenses/by-sa/4.0>, via Wikimedia Commons: https://commons.wikimedia.org/wiki/File:Muscovy_ducks_outside.jpg

Characteristics

Muscovy duck is a unique breed that can be spotted miles away because of their distinctive look. Their bodies are heavy, thick, and strong. Their feet are wide-set, long webbed that makes them waddle. Muscovy ducks, like turkeys and gobbles, have bumpy skin-like markings on their face. Furthermore, their bill is long and sloping in nature.

The male and the female Muscovy grow to the same height. Their height is around 26 to 33 inches, while their wingspan grows from 54 to 60 inches based on the duck's height.

The Muscovy duck has a fluctuating weight, mostly in adulthood, based on their habitat and the food they consume. The average body weight of the drake is around 4.6 to 6.8kg. Although the big, domesticated drakes weigh up to 8kg, the ducks weigh 5kg.

Needs

Your ducks need to be sheltered from predators and other elements. Ensure the shelter is well-ventilated to avoid any respiratory issues and large enough for them to roam freely.

Muscovy ducks enjoy roosting and perching, so make perches using wood or metal placed at various heights in the shelter. Put a nest box in the shelter to allow female Muscovy ducks to lay their eggs. Since they need access to water, they build their shelter close to a water source, a pond, a large dish of water, or a shallow pool.

Feed them with commercial feed and supplement their diet with fruits, vegetables, and greens.

Unique Value

Based on their versatile nature, Muscovy ducks have benefits ranging from pets to food production and agricultural uses. They are reared mainly due to their meat and egg production. This duck is handy when controlling pests, composting, and being kept as pets.

Temperament

Muscovy ducks are gentle and friendly to have as pets. They welcome the attention of both their owners and guests because they are not easily afraid or threatened by the presence of people.

Egg Production

These ducks are not a major producer of eggs. They can lay over 80 to 120 eggs yearly and hatch and raise four sets of Muscovy ducklings yearly. Their eggs are much larger than those of other breeds and tastier than chickens', making them a more favored choice for cooking.

Meat Production

This is where Muscovy ducks thrive the most. Their meat is very tasty and tender compared to veal and beef. Their breast meat is lean, and their skin contains less fat underneath it compared to other duck breeds.

Foraging Ability

Their foraging ability is top-notch. They can easily hunt for food when given the room, making them great for pest control.

Adaptability

This duck can adjust to any climate based on its hardy nature and ability to fly.

Aylesbury Ducks

The Aylesbury duck is a pink duck whose primary purpose is meat production. It is considered a backyard/ornamental bird due to its beautiful appearance and friendly nature. It is a domestic breed from the United Kingdom. The duck was developed in Aylesbury in Buckinghamshire, England, in the early 18th century.

The Aylesbury duck is considered a backyard/ornamental bird due to its beautiful appearance and friendly nature.

Jim Linwood, CC BY 2.0 <https://creativecommons.org/licenses/by/2.0>, via Wikimedia Commons: https://commons.wikimedia.org/wiki/File:Aylesbury_Ducks.jpg

Characteristics

Aylesbury is a big-sized duck breed. It has white skin and a thick white plumage that uniquely sets it apart from other domestic breeds.

They have a horizontal carriage and a long body. Their keel is straight, deep, and almost touching the ground. The Aylesbury has a long, straight, pinkish-white bill with legs and feet colored orange. It has a boat-shaped body due to the placement of its legs midway to the body, and it stands upside down parallel to the ground. They have swan-like long and thin necks with dark grayish-blue colored eyes.

Aylesbury ducks are of two types: the exhibition type and the utility type. The exhibition type has a deep keel, which makes it hard to mate naturally. The utility has a smaller keel, allowing them to mate successfully naturally. The average weight of the Aylesbury drake is about 5 kg, while the duck averages 4.5kg.

Needs

Aylesbury needs feed with many grains like barley, wheat, etc., and protein feeds such as fish meal. Additionally, it needs clean water, so put a container in their enclosure. Better still, you can let them free-range around ponds and other water sources as they enjoy foliage.

Unique Value

Aylesbury is primarily raised for meat production. Aylesbury are great companions if you are looking for a friendly and easy-to-manage pet. They are great for small spaces and can bring beauty to your garden. These ducks will make you smile by entertaining you with how they constantly chase each other. These ducks protect against mosquitoes as they excel at controlling mosquitoes in your backyard or garden. With their ranger ability to look for slugs, your backyard would be free of any stinging insects.

Temperament

Aylesbury is friendly and docile towards humans. They are sociable and enjoy being in groups. Feel free to let them socialize with other ducks in your home, but be careful of the drakes. They are capable of mating with any duck they encounter.

Egg Production

Aylesbury can produce eggs, but it's not something you should count on if you are into commercial farming. Within a year, a female's average egg production is 35 to 125 eggs.

Meat Production

Aylesbury is mainly known for its meat production, so they are reared as utility birds.

Foraging Ability

Aylesbury has an excellent foraging ability and, when allowed to roam, can cater for some of their feeds.

Adaptability

Aylesbury duck has a strong tolerance for all climates.

With these breeds in mind, choosing the right one for you should not be hard.

Chapter 4: Housing Your Ducks

If you're just starting out with raising ducks, creating the ideal housing and environment for them can seem daunting. Though relatively easy animals to handle and maintain, ducks have specific needs for shelter and protection. They require safe spaces to be shielded from potential predators and unpredictable weather. Whether you house your ducks within an existing structure or construct a dedicated duck coop, the key is providing them with security, nourishment, and enough space to move freely.

This chapter will guide you through the process of designing, building, and maintaining a duck coop or enclosure that caters to your ducks' specific needs. You'll find valuable insights into constructing a secure and cozy space for your feathered companions, with tips on design variations inspired by popular structures. By the end of this chapter, you'll be well-prepared to create a habitat that protects your ducks and enhances their overall quality of life, ensuring they thrive in their new environment. Whether you're a novice duck owner or an experienced enthusiast, the knowledge you gain here will contribute to the well-being and happiness of your beloved duck flock.

Ducks, though relatively easy animals to handle and maintain, do have specific needs for shelter and protection.

https://www.pexels.com/photo/herd-of-ducks-in-coop-11700747/

You don't necessarily need a full-scale barn to ensure safe and comfortable housing for your ducks. In fact, you can create a suitable living area on your property or even use a separate building for just this purpose. Whether you opt for a do-it-yourself (DIY) approach to building a duck coop or consider purchasing a pre-made enclosure, there are several critical elements to take into account before making a decision.

1. **DIY vs. Pre-made**: Decide whether you want to build your duck coop from scratch or purchase a pre-made one. DIY coops offer customization options but require more time and effort. Pre-made coops can save you time but may have limitations in terms of size and design.

2. **Location:** Choose a suitable location for your duck coop. It should be well-drained to prevent waterlogging, easily accessible for feeding and cleaning, and ideally situated to provide protection from prevailing winds.

3. **Size and Design**: Consider the size of your duck flock when designing or choosing a coop. Ducks need ample space to move around, so ensure the coop is roomy enough to accommodate them comfortably. A good rule of thumb is to allow at least 3-4 square feet of indoor space per duck.

4. **Materials:** Whether you're building or buying, select materials that are durable, weather-resistant, and easy to clean. Common choices include wood, plastic, and metal. Ensure the coop materials are safe for your ducks, as some treated wood or paints can be toxic.

5. **Roofing and Flooring:** Use a sturdy roofing material to keep your ducks dry, and consider adding an overhang to protect the coop's entrance from rain. A solid, easy-to-clean surface like concrete or wooden slats works well for flooring. Provide plenty of bedding material for insulation and comfort.

6. **Ventilation:** Proper ventilation is crucial to maintain air quality and prevent moisture buildup, which can lead to respiratory issues. Install vents and windows with screens to ensure good airflow.

7. **Security:** Ducks are vulnerable to predators like raccoons and weasels. Ensure your coop has secure locks and sturdy wire mesh on windows and openings to prevent unauthorized access.

8. **Accessibility:** Make sure the coop is designed for easy access for cleaning, egg collection, and daily care. Adequate access doors and ramps for ducks to move in and out are essential.

9. **Insulation**: Depending on your climate, you may need to insulate the coop to regulate temperature extremes. This is especially important if you live in an area with cold winters.

10. **Cost and Budget**: Consider your budget when planning your coop. DIY projects may be more cost-effective but require more time and effort. Pre-made coops offer convenience but may be pricier.

11. **Future Expansion**: If you plan to increase your duck flock in the future, design or select a coop that can accommodate growth without major modifications.

What Do You Need for Your Duck Coop?

With ducks, build a cage firm enough to keep them secluded in an area with enough water and straw under their feet, and they're good to go. When building a structure, use a wooden box or an old dog house at least 3 feet high and 4 feet in length and width.

The coops should be placed directly on the ground with enough room for future adjustments. In addition, ask yourself relevant questions like "How many ducks do I plan on raising?" and "For what reason exactly?" People raise ducks for many reasons, such as meat, eggs, and pets. No matter your purpose, you should consider the following elements.

1. Ventilation Is Vital

Ducks engage in certain habits that may lead to a less-than-pristine living environment. They tend to sleep on the ground, often leaving behind a trail of droppings right where they rest. Additionally, ducks typically make a beeline for their nests after a swim, not minding their damp and sometimes muddy state. It's crucial to understand these behaviors and take steps to maintain a healthy and hygienic living space for your ducks.

Proper ventilation is very important when customizing your ducks' shelter.

When providing shelter for your ducks, consider the following:

- **Proper Ventilation**: Adequate ventilation is essential to prevent the buildup of moisture in their sleeping areas, which can lead to health issues. Make sure that your coop has well-placed vents to allow for the circulation of fresh air. Positioning the ventilation area closer to the roofline helps maintain good air quality.

- **Coop Height**: Ideally, the coop's height should be around 3 feet to accommodate your ducks comfortably. This height provides ample space and allows for better air circulation.

By guaranteeing these aspects, you give your ducks access to clean and uncontaminated air, promoting their well-being and reducing the risk of illness.

2. Protection Against Predators

Ducks are vulnerable to a variety of predators, ranging from wild dogs, raccoons, foxes, wolves, bears, hawks, wild cats, and cougars to even domestic dogs. These opportunistic predators are drawn to the delectable taste of ducks, making it crucial to take proactive measures to safeguard your feathered friends.

Here are effective strategies to shield your ducks from potential threats:

- **Reinforce Enclosures**: Create fortified enclosures with sturdy walls and doors equipped with multiple latches. This provides an initial layer of protection. In rural settings with minimal predator presence, you can also consider using chicken wire as a cost-effective alternative, although it may be less secure.

- **Urban and Forested Areas**: If you're raising ducks in an urban or forested environment where predators are more prevalent, invest in a robust protection system. Consider wired electric fences or heavy-duty fencing to deter potential threats. Additionally, employing a livestock guarding dog can significantly enhance the security of your duck flock.

- **Scale According to Needs**: Tailor your protection measures to the scale of your duck-raising operation. If you have just one duck or a small number, strategically place your coop where you can easily access it. While this may seem simpler, it's crucial to prioritize safety even with a modest duck population.

Remember, the safety of your ducks is paramount, and the level of protection you choose should align with the potential risks in your specific environment. By implementing these strategies, you can guarantee the well-being of your ducks and enjoy peace of mind as you raise them.

3. Bedding and Nesting

When preparing a nesting area for your ducks, you need to select the right bedding materials for their comfort and hygiene. Opt for dry, organic materials with excellent absorbent qualities. Suitable choices include:

- Straw
- Hay
- Wood shavings
- Cedar shavings
- Shredded papers
- Chopped leaves
- Pine needles

When preparing a nesting area for your ducks, you need to select the right bedding materials for their comfort and hygiene.

Make sure you have an ample supply of these materials on hand for easy replacement whenever your ducks make a mess. While changing the bedding daily is unnecessary, it's advisable to remove soiled bedding every few days.

Instead of discarding the used bedding, consider repurposing it as compost for your garden. This eco-friendly practice reduces waste and enriches your garden soil with valuable nutrients, ultimately benefiting your ducks and plants.

By following these guidelines, you can create a clean and cozy nesting environment for your ducks, all while promoting sustainability in your gardening practices.

4. Good Location

One of the key advantages of having a portable and mobile coop is the ease with which you can disassemble and reassemble it when needed for location changes. Coop mobility becomes essential when adapting to changing weather conditions and ensuring the well-being of your ducks.

Consider these scenarios where portable coops shine:

- **Weather Adaptation:** In the face of changing weather patterns, such as excessive sun or harsh winter conditions, you can effortlessly relocate your coop. For example, during scorching summers, moving the coop to a shadier, cooler area with access to fresh water ensures your ducks stay comfortable. Conversely, relocating to a warmer spot in colder months provides essential protection.

- **Preventing Dead Spots:** Regularly shifting the coop prevents your backyard or garden from developing unsightly dead spots. This mobility fosters healthier soil quality and contributes to a more vibrant environment for your ducks to thrive.

The continuous adaptability of a portable coop not only enhances your ducks' living conditions but also positively impacts the soil quality, creating an ideal setting for their growth and well-being.

5. Spacing per Duck

If you plan on raising more than one duck, you'll have to be certain each one has at least 3-5 square feet in the coop. Multiply 3-5 square feet by the number of ducks you plan on raising and see how much spacing you will need.

6. Build a Larger Duck Coop than Needed

Constructing a duck coop doesn't have to be an expensive endeavor. In fact, you can make the most out of leftover materials from previous projects to create a thrifty yet efficient duck shelter. Here's how to optimize your coop-building process:

- **Resourceful Recycling**: Gather any leftover scraps from past repairs or projects in your yard. These seemingly insignificant leftovers can be ingeniously combined to craft a functional duck coop. This not only saves on costs but also reduces waste.

- **Plan for Expansion:** Embrace the idea of potential growth in your duck-raising venture. Consider building a larger coop than currently needed, with expansion in mind. While it may seem unconventional, trust in the process and anticipate future changes. Begin with a minimum of 4 square feet of flooring per duck, and plan to expand to 12 square feet as your flock grows. This approach caters to your present requirements and positions you favorably if you decide to accommodate additional ducks later on.

By adopting these strategies, you can construct a cost-effective duck coop that serves your immediate needs while allowing room for future expansion while making the most of available resources.

Unique Coop Designs for Your Ducks

If you're planning to raise multiple ducks, it's essential to consider the right coop structures to accommodate them comfortably. Whether you choose to make them yourself or order pre-made coops, adequate space is key. Here are some innovative duck coop designs to inspire your duck-keeping venture:

1. Tyrant Quacker Box

- The Tyrant coop can house up to six ducks, offering mobility with its wheels and making location changes hassle-free.

- This design features a nesting box measuring 3 feet high, 3 feet wide, and 4 feet long, topped with a removable, waterproof green roof.

- The coop incorporates approximately 1-inch galvanized wire mesh to deter predators, which is especially effective in safeguarding ducklings.

- The Tyrant Quacker Box proves to be an efficient choice for duck protection and care.

2. Artisan Urban Coop

- Designed with urban settings in mind, this mobile coop features wheels for easy maneuverability.

- The coop structure utilizes chicken wire for ventilation and includes a cozy, dog-sized house for your ducks' comfort and safety.

- Its mobility allows you to shift it effortlessly, preserving grass and enhancing soil health.

DIY Artisan Coop

If you're inclined to build your own Artisan-style coop, here's a basic guide:

Materials required: Plywood, nails, screws, wood glue, metal sheets for roofing, hinges, latches, wire mesh, hardware cloth, paint or sealant, pressured timber, and roosting bars.

1. Begin by planning the coop's size based on your duck count, allocating approximately 3-4 square feet per duck.

2. Create a foundation using pressured 2×4 wood, building a balanced, square, rectangular frame aligned with your layout plan.

3. Establish vertical supports for the coop walls and attach the rectangular frame securely.

4. Frame the top and bottom of the walls using horizontal 2x4s, considering space for doors, vents, and windows.

5. Construct a simple yet effective roof frame from 2×4s, attaching it to the coop walls.

6. Add nesting boxes to the roof using plywood, each with a 12' width and 12' length, and a sloped roof for drainage.

7. Install a 2×2 roosting bar above the floor inside the coop.

8. Create openings for ventilation and windows in the walls, covering them with mesh wires or hardware cloth for predator protection.

9. Install a convenient access door and a ramp for ducks to enter and exit the coop.

10. Cover the roof frame with waterproof and weather-resistant metal sheets or shingles.

11. Apply non-toxic, mild paint to the exterior to safeguard your coop from the elements.

3. Promise Land Duck Wagon

The Promise Land Wagon is a spacious and portable coop solution for your ducks, designed to be pulled by a small tractor or an ATV.

Its metal roofing incorporates a gutter system to efficiently collect and store water, with a substantial 65-gallon capacity.

This coop grants your ducks the freedom to roam your property without the constant search for water sources.

4. Green Willows

The Green Willows A-framed coop offers versatility to accommodate various flock sizes.

You can easily customize its dimensions to suit your needs. For example, an 8x6x6-foot structure suits around 10 ducks, while expanding to 10x8x7 feet provides ample space for about 15 ducks.

This design is straightforward to build and mobile, allowing your ducks to move freely. It offers ample nesting, bedding, feeding, and watering areas.

Building a DIY Green Willows Design
Materials

- Wired mesh
- Bamboo sticks or thatch for roofing
- Recycled hinges and latches
- Sustainable wood
- Saw, drills, hammer, and nails
- Natural paints or sealants
- Measuring tape

Procedure
Construction Steps:

1. Begin by sketching a layout that incorporates gentle curves and a natural, harmonious aesthetic with your surroundings. Utilize recycled materials and sustainable wood to minimize costs.

2. Craft a curved or undulating base frame resembling the graceful flow of a willow tree. Ensure all points are balanced and aligned.

3. Add vertical wooden supports to the base frame, securing them with screws or nails, leaving space for windows and ventilation.

4. Install the roofing using bamboo sticks or thatched panels for their safety, sustainability, and natural look.

5. Create a central circular area within the coop for nesting and bedding, constructing sustainable wooden nesting boxes with sloped roofs to facilitate egg collection.

6. Cover ventilation openings with wire mesh or eco-friendly fencing to ensure proper airflow while keeping predators at bay.

7. Build a ramp with reclaimed or sustainable wood, attaching it securely to the coop's entrance to help ducks easily access it. Test the ramp for safety.

8. Apply natural paints or sealants to protect the wood from the elements. Line the coop's interior with straw and hay for bedding.

9. Place your Green Willows coop in a suitable spot within your backyard or chosen location.

10. Regularly inspect the coop for repairs or upgrades and maintain its natural ambiance to extend its lifespan.

5. Hill Homestead With Flat Mobile Coop

The Hill Homestead design offers a rectangular and practical mobile coop solution if you're budget-conscious.

Outfitted with chicken wire mesh, metal roofing, and a single or double-hinged door, this coop is compact and easy to move without needing a tractor or ATV.

These innovative coop designs provide excellent options for raising ducks, catering to various needs, budgets, and preferences. Choose the one that best suits your situation and confidently embark on your duck-raising adventure.

Tips on Maintaining a Safe and Clean Coop

Keeping your ducklings healthy and secure while maintaining their living environment is paramount. Proper hygiene helps prevent fungal infections and diseases, and safeguarding them from predators is equally essential. To ensure your duck-raising venture thrives, consider these professional tips:

1. Start Small for a Smooth Beginning

- If you're new to duck farming, begin with a small flock, perhaps five ducklings, to familiarize yourself with the basics. Once you gain confidence and expertise, you can gradually expand your flock.

- Carefully plan and research the resources, time commitment, and potential challenges involved, such as theft, predators, and regulatory permits. Starting small also minimizes the cleanup effort required for larger flocks.

2. Social Ducks Are Happy Ducks

- Ducks are social creatures, much like chickens. If you're new to duck-keeping, having at least two ducklings to provide companionship is advisable.

- Consider getting ducks of the same sex (pairs of females or males) to prevent potential breeding complications.

3. No-Tip Bowls for Food and Water

- Ducks love water and tend to be a bit clumsy with their sideways-set eyes. Use no-tip bowls for food and water to minimize spills and mess.

- Craft or purchase no-tip water containers that keep their bowls consistently filled, ensuring a steady supply of clean water day and night.

4. Choose Low Dust Bedding

- Opt for low-dust wood shavings like Aspen as bedding for your ducklings' brooder. These shavings are odor-free, highly absorbent, soft, and free from pest contaminants.

- Using low-dust bedding ensures clean air quality in the coop and reduces the need for frequent cleaning due to dust buildup.

5. Use Pellet Food and Keep It Separate

- Pelletized food is an excellent option for duck feed, offering three variations: Mash (unprocessed feed), Pellets (steamed and formed kibbles), and Crumbles (derived from pellets with a powdery texture).

- Pellets are ideal, especially if you want to minimize waste and mess. Separate the feed and water bowls to prevent contamination and maintain cleanliness.

6. Maintain Predator Defense

- Ducks are appealing prey for predators, especially in rural areas. Implement robust predator defense methods to safeguard your flock.

- Regularly inspect and reinforce coop security to deter potential threats.

In this comprehensive guide, you've discovered DIY coop designs, maintenance tips, and essential insights for raising happy and healthy ducks. By prioritizing hygiene, safety, and the well-being of your ducks, you'll embark on a rewarding journey of duck farming with confidence.

Chapter 5: Duck Nutrition: What to Feed Them

Like humans, ducks have nutritional needs for every stage of their lives. For instance, ducklings require higher protein levels than adult ducks because they are still developing and growing.

Ducks' dietary needs also differ depending on their purpose. If you raise them for meat production, they will need a different diet from the ones you are raising for eggs.

Whether your ducks are loving pets or a source of food, they need a balanced diet to live a long and healthy life.

This chapter explains in detail duck nutrition, various feeding types and their pros and cons, risks of malnutrition, and safe treats to give your ducks.

Ducklings require higher protein levels than adult ducks because they are still developing and growing.

https://unsplash.com/photos/cyG0m2JpL8Y

Nutritional Needs for Every Stage of the Duck's Life

You should feed your ducks food appropriate for their age and needs. Like babies, there are certain types of food that ducklings won't handle until they are fully grown.

Three Weeks and Younger

Ducks three weeks and younger should eat crumbles that are high in protein. They need plenty of protein (about 18-20%) at this stage of their life because they are still developing. However, you shouldn't chicken-feed them as this type doesn't have enough vitamin B3 and other nutrients ducks crucially need at this young age.

Three to Twenty Weeks

At this stage, feed your ducks high-quality food that aids growth. The food should either be for ducks or young chickens. Since their needs are changing, lower protein levels to 15%.

Twenty Weeks and Older

Now that your duck is a full-grown adult, it will require a different diet. Feed them breeder food or a high-quality layer that is suitable for adult chickens or ducks. There are many options to choose from, but mixed grains and pellets are your best options. Suppose you are raising ducks for their eggs. In that case, you must pay extra attention to their diet because nutritional deficiencies can cause various diseases and render their eggs inedible. They will usually need a daily dose of calcium to produce strong eggs. Try shell grit since it contains about 38% calcium.

You can also give them a commercial diet with the appropriate amount of fruits and vegetables.

Now that you understand how to feed your duck based on age, you need to learn how to provide a balanced diet filled with the necessary proteins, vitamins, and minerals.

Proteins

When people hear the word protein, the first thing that often comes to mind is meat, poultry, or fish. However, ducks don't require the same type of proteins that humans or animals consume. They just need the amino acids that exist in proteins. Amino acids are necessary for ducks' growth and can protect their health in every stage of their lives.

Similar to humans, ducks require about twenty-two types of amino acids every day. Some of them are produced naturally inside of their bodies, while they can only get the others from eating food high in proteins.

To guarantee that your duck will grow properly and healthily, feed it food containing these amino acids.

Methionine

Methionine is one of the most essential amino acids you should include in your ducks' diet. You can find it in cereal grains, Brazilian nuts, sesame seeds, eggs, and fish. There is also a supplement called DL-methionine that you can give to your ducks in organic feed. However, if you don't want to give your duck chemicals and prefer to stick to a natural diet, only focus on foods that contain methionine rather than giving them supplements.

Give ducklings up to two weeks old about 0.70% of methionine. During their growing period, reduce it to 0.55, and then 50% during their breeding age.

Lysine

According to a study published by Dr. Ariane Helmbrecht, a specialist in animal nutrition, ducks need at least 1% of lysine amino acid for their development. When they are three weeks old or less, they require high levels of lysine to speed up their growth and reduce the risk of any health issues. After this period, they will only need between 0.7 and 0.95%. Lysine is usually found in soybeans, fish, hemp seeds, pumpkin seeds, shellfish, eggs, and snails.

Arginine

If you raise ducks for their meat, feed them food containing arginine. This amino acid can increase their weight without needing to feed them extra meals. You can find arginine in dairy products, brown rice, buckwheat, cereals, corn, oats, sunflower seeds, and sesame seeds. Meat ducks only require 1% of arginine.

Vitamins and Minerals

Ducks need to be exposed to the sun regularly to get their vitamin D needs. However, some areas don't usually get enough sunlight, especially during the winter. In this case, you must provide your duck with Vitamin D, specifically Vitamin D3, through food or supplements. A Vitamin D deficiency can lead to many health issues like weak eggshells and bones. If your duck has low levels of phosphorus or calcium, you can make it up by increasing their Vitamin D intake. Kelp contains high levels of Vitamin D, so include it in your duck's diet.

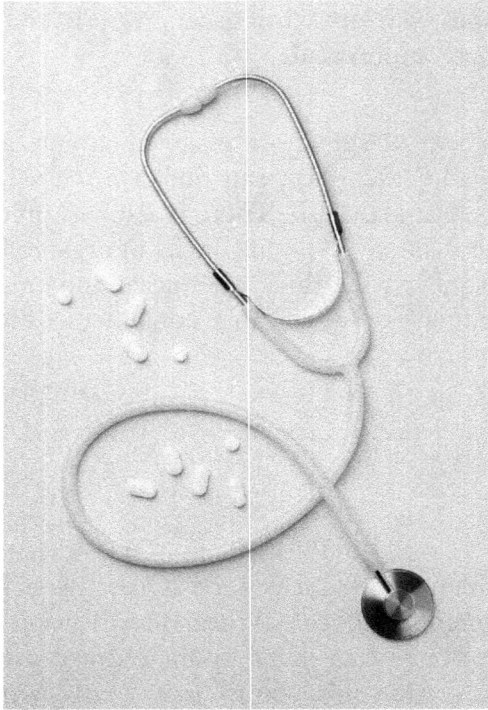

Just like humans, ducks need their vitamins in order to grow and be healthy.
https://www.pexels.com/photo/yellow-stethoscope-and-medicines-on-pink-background-4047077/

Your ducks also need Vitamin A and calcium for their health and development. You can usually find them in formulated foods, vegetables, and greens. Weak eggshells are a clear sign of calcium deficiency. Monitoring your duck's eggs is necessary as they can tell you so much about their health. Calcium supplements will strengthen the ducks' bones and eggshells and protect them against osteoporosis and reproductive diseases.

Laying ducks need more calcium than meat ducks. If you want your duck to lay healthy eggs, feed them food with high calcium levels, like sunflower seeds.

Your duck will also require a regular intake of Vitamin E to improve their immune system. Include greens in their diet; this is much easier if you have a yard or a small garden.

Grains are a great source of Vitamin E, Vitamin B, and Phosphorus as well. Give your ducks whole grains, corn, or oats, but avoid getting them wet, as they can be poisonous for them.

Niacin, commonly known as Vitamin B3, is vital for your duck's health. In fact, they require a much higher level of niacin in their diet than chicken. Therefore, chicken feed for your ducks isn't recommended since they won't get adequate Vitamin B3.

Niacin can improve the ducks' blood circulation, nervous system, digestion, feathers, and skin health. It is necessary to feed your duck food rich in niacin from a very young age regularly. Vitamin B3 converts carbohydrates, fats, and other nutrients into energy. This process can lower cholesterol, protect them from diabetes, and improve their muscle tone.

Ducklings require a daily dose of 10 mg of niacin, and adult ducks require 12.5 mg per day. Food containing niacin includes sunflower seeds, pumpkin, feeder fish, sardines, salmon, tuna fish, whole wheat, peanuts, sweet potatoes, and peas.

Niacin deficiency is extremely serious and can lead to many health issues like diarrhea, loss of appetite, slow growth, joint and leg problems that can affect movements, and in some severe cases, it can be fatal.

Ducks require other types of minerals in their diet to improve their growth rate, increase their weight, and aid in producing high-quality eggs.

- Selenium
- Iron
- Manganese
- Zinc
- Copper
- Potassium
- Sodium
- Cobalt
- Iodine
- Magnesium
- Chlorine

Many types of food are rich in minerals, like widgeon grass, southern naiad, pondweed, milfoil, coontail, wild celery, wild rice, and other aquatic plants.

Clean Water

All living creatures need clean and fresh water to survive, and ducks are no different. Your ducks should have access to clean water all day. Whether you are raising them for companionship, their eggs, or meat, they mustn't go for more than eight hours without water. Lack of water can be dangerous for their health. It can affect their mental and physical health as they can exhibit signs of stress, anxiety, and destructive behavior.

Ducks and ducklings don't only need water for drinking, but they love to bathe and go swimming as well. Think of your duck as a little child who will get excited whenever it sees water and wants to jump in right away. However, don't let your duckling go swimming until it reaches two weeks old.

You can place an artificial pond for them in your backyard so they can have access to swimming and exercise all day. Keep the pool clean by regularly removing dead plants and leaves and draining the water.

The Pros and Cons of Various Feeding Types

There are various ways to feed your ducks. Choose the method you are comfortable with that fits your environment and financial situation. This part of the chapter focuses on the pros and cons of the most common feeding types.

Foraging

Foraging or free range allows your ducks to explore their environment and find their own food. Some people believe that it is unhealthy to feed your duck because you won't be able to provide them with all the nutrients they need. Foraging comes easy for them since it's in their nature to search and hunt for food. They will get their nutritional needs from flies, worms, beetles, slugs, and snails. In fact, a duck will happily choose a bug over regular feeding or any other source of protein you give them.

Foraging or free range allows your ducks to explore their environment and find their own food.
https://pixabay.com/photos/duck-mallard-bird-nature-wildlife-899078/

Pros of Foraging

Gives Them a Chance to Exercise

Ducks are extroverts. They like to be in groups to socialize and quack about different topics. Foraging allows them to spend time with each other to exercise, bond, and look for food. They can move around and stay active instead of being confined in a small space. Ducks prefer looking for food over being served every meal. When you let them forage, you allow them to be in their natural habitat. On the other hand, ducks in confined spaces are usually stressed and can suffer from various health issues. Ducks that forage are much healthier and happier.

Protects Them against Diseases

Active ducks are less likely to get sick. When ducks are in confined places, they don't get enough exercise and are usually in close proximity to other ducks, leading them to contract diseases from each other. Foraging also exposes ducks to sunlight and fresh air, which is necessary for their well-being.

Provides Them with More Protein Intake

Although commercial feed can provide ducks with protein, a foraging diet is much richer in proteins that they can easily find in bugs and other insects.

Better for the Environment

Unlike commercial feed that uses fungicides, herbicides, pesticides, and harmful chemicals, foraging is better for the environment. Foraging is a natural method that can keep your ducks healthy and protect green areas in your city.

Protects Grass and Lawn

Foraging protects your lawn and grass from damage. When ducks have little space to roam, they will only walk on the lawn and kill your grass. If you have many ducks, their waste can also ruin your plants. When you allow them to forage, they can move around in large spaces, so their waste won't be an issue since it will be distributed in various areas, and they won't focus on a small part of the land.

Controls Insects

Since your ducks will eat the bugs in your backyard or garden, the number of insects will decrease drastically. They can also hunt rats and mice to reduce the pest problem in your home.

Saves Money

Instead of spending money on commercial feed, let your ducks forage for their food. You'll end up saving a lot of money.

It Is More Humane

Animals and birds shouldn't be confined in small spaces. They should have ample space in nature to move freely. Foraging is more humane because it puts the ducks in their natural habitat, making them healthier, happier, and less stressed and bored. Confinement can cause ducks to exhibit unhealthy behavior, like biting their skin and plucking their feathers.

Cons of Foraging

Predators

Foraging exposes ducks to predators like dogs, foxes, and owls. Placing a fence and net isn't always helpful. So, if you live in an area populated with wild animals, consider another feeding type.

Escaping

If something happens that frightens or stresses your duck, it may run off and never come back! They can also fly away, making it hard for you to catch them. If you can't keep your ducks safe, foraging may not be a good idea.

Damage Flowers

Ducks will eat any type of plant in your backyard, including flowers. So, if you have a flower garden, they will destroy it.

Home-Mixed Feed vs. Commercial Feed

Commercial feed offers your duck store-made food, usually made of by-products and cereal grains. Home-mixed is mixing various types of food to prepare a nutritional meal for your ducks. Most people struggle with choosing between home-mixed feed and commercial feed. You certainly want to keep your ducks healthy, but there are many things you should consider.

Pros of Home-Mixed Feed

- More beneficial than commercial feed
- Filled with more nutrients
- Cheaper than commercial feed
- Doesn't contain chemicals

Cons of Home-Mixed Feed

- Time-consuming
- If you aren't aware of the proper nutrients, you won't be able to prepare a healthy meal and cause malnutrition.

Pros of Commercial Feed

- Easy and cheap (Read the label to make sure it has everything your duck needs)
- High levels of protein
- Contains minerals and vitamins

Cons of Commercial Feed

- May not always meet your duck's nutritional needs
- Can contain chemicals or additives
- More expensive than foraging and home-mixed feed
- Contains pesticides that can cause cancer

The Risk of Malnutrition in Ducks

Ducks can suffer from malnutrition if they don't get the necessary nutrients. In fact, it is the leading cause of death among ducks. Malnutrition can affect their immune system and cause various health problems.

Feather Plucking

Feather plucking is often a clear sign that a duck is suffering from malnutrition. They are either not getting enough protein or getting too much fat and carbohydrates. If ducks aren't getting enough minerals or vitamins, they will pluck or chew their feathers. In some severe cases, they can chew off all of them. Featherless ducks are prone to infections and skin ulcerations.

Diarrhea or Constipation

Malnutrition can cause diarrhea, constipation, or even both at the same time. Their stools can be soft and more frequent, or you will notice small dry droppings here and there. Diarrhea and constipation are clear signs that you need to change your diet. Contact your vet right away so they can run the necessary tests and recommend the appropriate nutrients or supplements.

Egg Binding

Egg binding occurs when the duck struggles with passing its eggs. Sometimes, they can be so large that they get stuck. This can cause serious infections or even death.

Lethargy

Similar to humans, if ducks are suffering from malnutrition, they will feel lethargic and sleepy. Remember, ducks are active creatures that don't like to sit still and enjoy socializing. So, if you notice their behavior changing, it is a sign that something isn't right.

Preventing Malnutrition in Ducks

Malnutrition can easily be avoided with these simple tips.

Feed Your Duck a Balanced Diet

A balanced diet is the best remedy against malnutrition. Feed your duck with the necessary fats, proteins, minerals, and vitamins. Give them the appropriate percentage for their age and needs. If you change their diet, but they aren't getting better, consult their vet, as they can recommend a better diet or supplements.

Clean Everything

Make sure to clean their artificial pond and to only provide them with fresh water. Their food should also be clean and fresh.

Provide Them with Physical Activity

Ducks aren't stagnant creatures. Provide them with the opportunity and space to exercise. If you live in a safe area, leave your ducks to forage for their food.

Avoid Junk Food

Junk food can affect your ducks' health and cause obesity and heart attacks. Avoid feeding them any food that doesn't have nutritional value, like crackers and bread.

Safe and Unsafe Treats and Foraging Plants

Express your love to your ducks by feeding them delicious treats. However, you should make sure that you only give them safe plants.

Safe Treats

- Uncooked worms
- Mealworms
- Dandelion
- Clover
- Fresh herbs
- Leafy greens like lettuce
- Grains
- Nuts
- Grass cuttings
- Cooked beans
- Cooked eggs
- Eggshells

Unsafe Treats

- Spinach
- Raw eggs
- Raw meat

- Bread
- Chocolate
- Caffeine
- Salty food
- Dried beans
- Green Potatoes
- Green tomatoes
- Raw potatoes
- Garlic
- Onions
- Rhubarb leaves
- Fruit seeds and pits

Safe Foraging Plants

- Wild violets
- Wild strawberries
- Smartweed
- Purslane
- Purple deadnettle
- Plantain
- Oxalis
- Mugwort
- Fat hen
- Dandelion
- Creeping Charlie
- Clover
- Avocado
- Tobacco
- Oat
- Potatoes
- Philodendron

- Nightshade
- Milkweed
- Foxglove
- Elephant ear
- Eggplant
- Coffee Bean
- Calla Lily
- Buttercup
- Black locust
- Avocado

Unsafe Forage Plants

- Oleander
- Oak trees
- Mountain Laurel
- Larkspur
- Clematis
- Castor bean
- Boxwood
- Ivy
- Pokeweed
- Honeysuckle
- Bleeding heart
- Azalea
- Yew
- Wisteria
- Rhododendron
- Daffodil
- Iris
- Buttercup
- Tulips

- Sweet peas
- Poppies
- Lupine
- Poppies

Raising ducks is a considerable responsibility. They are living creatures that require constant care and attention. You should learn their nutritional requirements based on their age and needs. This is specifically necessary if you are going to feed them home-mixed food. For commercial feed, read the label on the food packages to check if they have sufficient proteins, minerals, and vitamins.

Ducks love water. They either drink it or swim in it. Place an artificial water pond or even a small swimming pool for your birds to swim and exercise. They should also have a large space because birds suffer in confinement. They can use this space to forage their food and get sunlight and fresh air. Foraging is one of the cheapest, healthiest, and most humane feeding types. However, if you don't have the time or space, you can choose between home-mixed or commercial feed.

Monitor your ducks' weight and habits to ensure they don't suffer from malnutrition. Prepare balanced meals and give them the necessary supplements to protect their health and prevent the risk of weak eggs or diseases. Finally, learn about safe and unsafe plants and treats to avoid accidents that can risk your bird's life.

Chapter 6: Duck Health and Wellness

Ducks' graceful movements and charming appearance are delightful additions to ponds, farms, and homesteads. Providing them with essential healthcare and wellness is crucial to improving their overall well-being, longevity, and productivity. While ducks may appear hardy and self-sufficient, they are not immune to the challenges that affect all living creatures. They can succumb to diseases, parasitic infections, and environmental stressors that compromise their health and well-being. Neglecting their healthcare can lead to suffering and reduced productivity.

The essence of this chapter lies in recognizing the vital role of proper duck healthcare and wellness. By gaining fundamental insights into their unique needs and vulnerabilities, you'll be equipped to be a responsible and caring steward of your feathered friends. This knowledge will enhance the ducks' overall well-being and longevity and maximize their productivity, whether through healthier egg-laying or pest control.

Common Health Issues

Respiratory Infections

Ducks suffering from respiratory infections can show signs of sneezing, nasal discharge, coughing, and experience difficulty breathing. With certain respiratory infections, you might even hear wheezing when they breathe in certain respiratory infections.

Make sure that their coop has proper ventilation to prevent moisture buildup. Besides cleaning the housing, keep the environment clean and dry, avoiding overcrowding. If the ducks have access to an artificial water body, clean it regularly to prevent the development of water-borne diseases like avian cholera. Provide ducks with a well-balanced diet to support their immune system.

Botulism

Ducks suffering from this toxin-releasing infection show signs of paralysis, weakness, and drooping of the neck, head, and wings. The Clostridium botulinum bacteria thrive in stagnant and contaminated water sources. Keeping the water source clean and uncontaminated will significantly prevent the development of botulism-causing bacteria. The containers that provide fresh drinking water should also be cleaned regularly to further inhibit disease-causing microorganisms' development. In severe cases, isolate the affected birds and provide supportive care if necessary.

Avian Influenza (Bird Flu)

Bird flu or avian influenza in ducks starts with clear signs of respiratory distress and reduced egg production. As the infection progresses, ducks might exhibit a swollen head and, in severe infections, can even face sudden death. Avian influenza is a viral infection. Therefore, it's imperative to follow biosecurity measures. Limit the ducks' contact with other wild animals or birds, keep the premises clean, and follow vaccination protocols implemented by relevant authorities. You should also notify your veterinarian and report the disease to authorities, as this highly contagious disease can spread like wildfire. Lastly, don't forget to minimize contact with other bird species, as most wild and poultry birds are potential carriers.

Duck Viral Enteritis (Duck Plague)

Ducks infected with duck viral enteritis will experience loss of appetite, an increase in depression, and greenish or blood-tinged diarrhea. In severe cases, viral enteritis can even result in sudden death. For the flock's safety, isolate new ducks before integrating them. Maintain a clean and sanitized environment to minimize the risk of disease transmission.

Parasitic Infections

Ducks suffering from parasitic infections exhibit mild to severe feather loss, significant weight loss, decreased egg production, and visible parasites on the feathers and skin. Regularly cleaning and disinfecting the duck housing is essential. Other preventative measures include giving the ducks access to dust where they can roll to naturally keep the parasites under control. You should also administer appropriate deworming treatments after consultation and supervision with the veterinarian.

Duck Cholera

Your ducks will start showing signs of lethargy, lose their appetite, and experience difficulty in breathing. Slowly, the joints will become swollen with progressively worsening symptoms. Maintaining a clean environment, like keeping their housing, water sources, and feeding areas clean, can keep duck cholera at bay. Veteran duck farmers suggest avoiding overcrowding and providing a well-balanced diet to strengthen the immune system and metabolic processes.

Aspergillosis

Ducks will show labored breathing, coughing, persistent nasal discharge, lethargy, and limited movement in this lung infection. The primary cause of aspergillosis development is high humidity. Keeping the housing ventilated, clean, and dry will prevent the growth of harmful fungi and other microorganisms.

Egg Binding

This is a common egg-laying-associated condition occurring in female ducks. The eggs fail to release through the oviduct in the female's reproductive system, pass through the maturation process, and complete the egg-laying process within the standard time. Ducks with this problem will show signs of lethargy and will make several visits to the nest due to abdominal straining.

Providing a calcium-rich diet is crucial to promote eggshell formation. Also, make comfortable nesting boxes and bedding and monitor the egg-laying behavior and frequency, as this information can be provided to the veterinarian for better diagnosis and treatment.

Leg and Foot Problems (Bumblefoot)

The most common limb-related problem with ducks is the bumblefoot. It's an abscess that forms at any area on the bird's footpad. It will start as a small, red, and inflamed bump that can deepen and increase in size. These bumps can also turn into lesions or sores, depending on their immunity levels and the cleanliness of the premises. The most evident sign of bumblefoot is the growth of these bumps or sores, which should be monitored and treated immediately.

If several ducks are affected by these bumps, immediately clean the flooring, replace the bedding, reduce humidity through adequate ventilation, and feed them a balanced diet to keep their immunity levels at optimum. However, if you are not seeing effective results, contacting a veterinarian and following their guideline can prevent this bacteria from spreading further.

Newcastle Disease

This is a highly contagious viral disease common in ducks, chickens, turkeys, and pigeons. It causes frequent sneezing, coughing, problems with digestion and production of greenish diarrhea, and neurological signs like paralysis and twisting of the neck. The female ducks affected by this viral disease also have reduced egg production.

Newcastle disease is a viral infection that spreads from the affected ducks to the rest of the flock. Therefore, always practice stringent biosecurity methods like quarantine and isolation to prevent disease spread. Lab tests can be done to confirm it before vaccinating.

Mycoplasma Induced Infections

Mycoplasma gallisepticum is a microorganism that causes chronic respiratory diseases in ducks and poultry birds. When fully developed, the disease causes decreased egg laying, persistent nasal discharge, coughing, sneezing, and inflammation around the eyes (conjunctivitis). Like any other disease, maintaining good hygiene can reduce the disease spread.

Duck Hepatitis

This is an acute viral infection primarily affecting ducklings under six weeks old. Duck viral hepatitis (DVH) has three subtypes and does not affect older birds. The ducks affected by the viral infection show jaundice (yellowing of eyes and skin beneath the fur), lethargy, and decreased food intake. DVH spreads in unsanitary environments, especially from water sources and already infected ducks. Isolating the infected ducks and minimizing overcrowding is crucial to minimizing the spread.

Regular monitoring is necessary as it can reveal signs of illness, behavioral changes, or any unusual symptoms. You can share the insights with a certified veterinarian for a better diagnosis and treatment. Following the required husbandry practices like keeping the housing clean, providing a balanced diet, and implementing biosecurity measures can significantly decrease the risk of several health issues and diseases.

Parasitic Infections (Internal and External)

While there are several parasitic infections, most show common signs of weight loss, decreased appetite, feather loss, and visible parasites on the feathers and skin in severe cases. Most parasitic infections can be decreased by improving sanitation, providing dust baths, deworming, and treating external parasites.

Parasitic Protozoa (Coccidiosis)

Coccidiosis is a parasitic disease found commonly in wild and farm ducks. This parasite reaches the duck's gut through contaminated food. The parasite lives within the gut, feeding and reproducing. Coccidiosis causes decreased appetite, lethargy, bloody diarrhea, and significant weight loss. It's best to consult a veterinarian for an appropriate treatment immediately. To minimize the outbreak, follow a regular cleaning schedule like disinfecting and cleaning the housing and providing them with fresh, healthy food.

Early detection, prompt intervention, and collaboration with a qualified avian veterinarian are essential for accurate diagnosis and effective treatment of these diseases and parasites. Implementing a comprehensive health management plan, including biosecurity measures, proper nutrition, and regular monitoring, will contribute to the overall well-being of your duck flock.

Maintaining Hygiene

Maintaining adequate hygiene is necessary to prevent disease spread and improve the health and wellness of your duck's flock. Here are some practices you can incorporate into the duck hygiene management routine.

Sanitize Living Areas

Disinfecting the housing, perches, feeding utensils, and nearby water sources. Don't let waste accumulate in a specific area. Replace wet or unsanitary bedding and leftover food to prevent the development of harmful microorganisms and pest attraction. Before using disinfectants or cleaners, make sure that the substances are safe for ducks.

Provide Clean Water

Providing fresh and clean water for both drinking and bathing is vital. Regularly changing the water prevents the growth of bacteria, contamination, and disease transmission, and it is free from contaminants like feces, droppings, and debris.

Proper Waste Management

Designate a water disposal area away from the duck living spaces where you can compost the leftover food or dispose of the waste while reducing disease transmission.

Implement Quarantine Procedures

As many viral infections are transmitted by contact with already infected ducks, implementing strict quarantine and monitoring practices can guarantee your flock's health. Whenever you want to add more ducks to the flock, quarantine them to prevent the introduction of potential diseases. Monitoring the quarantined ducks for any signs of illness is done during quarantine.

Biosecurity Measures

When introducing ducks to a new place, follow biosecurity measures and limit visitor interactions, especially with people in contact with other poultry birds like turkeys and chickens. Likewise, limit their access to wild birds as they are potential carriers and transmitters of avian diseases. If your ducks suffer from an ongoing disease, outbreak, or infection, make sure that all visitors and caretakers use sanitized clothing and feasible footwear and follow biosecurity protocols to contain the disease's spread.

Maintain Dry Conditions

Keep the housing area dry and prevent standing water through regular cleaning. Keeping the area ventilated, especially in humid conditions, will limit the growth of bacteria.

Dust Baths

Dust bathing is a natural method practiced by ducks to remove external parasites, keep their feathers clean, and prevent the development of skin-related diseases.

Foot and Hand Hygiene

Besides caring for the duck flock, maintain adequate foot and hand hygiene after handling and feeding them. Use foot baths with added disinfectant when entering and exiting the duck area to minimize disease transmission.

Provide a Balanced Diet

To keep your ducks healthy and thriving, adequate nutrition must be provided to strengthen the immune system, increase metabolism, and keep the body ready to fight an infection or a disease.

Education and Training

The diseases and conditions shared here are the most common ones, but there are several other diseases you should be familiar with as a caretaker. Reading more, joining duck farming communities, talking with duck farmers, and sharing your passion can increase disease knowledge. For better understanding, you can discuss the symptoms, preventative measures, and treatment protocol with other duck farmers.

Attending workshops and discussing disease-related issues with an avian veterinarian will also enhance your ability to promptly address these diseases and infections. Integrating these hygiene practices into your duck management routine allows you to create a clean and disease-resistant environment and contribute to the health and longevity of your flock.

Seeking Veterinary Help

It's necessary to understand when to seek veterinary assistance. You need to look out for several red flags as they indicate an underlying illness, disease, or a medical condition that might require veterinarian assistance.

Unusual Behavior

Ducks' behavior changes significantly when they suffer from a disease or a medical condition. They will become less active, avoid interaction, isolate themselves, or exhibit aggressive behavior. These are some signs that something might be wrong with their health. Consulting a veterinarian can help identify and address any underlying issues causing these behavior changes.

Respiratory Infection Symptoms

Ducks, like all animals, can suffer from respiratory infections. It could indicate respiratory issues if you notice symptoms such as frequent sneezing, coughing, labored breathing, nasal discharge, or unusual sounds when they breathe. Seeking veterinary assistance is vital to diagnose the cause and provide appropriate treatment to prevent further complications.

Digestive Issues

Ducks exhibiting persistent diarrhea, changes in appetite, constipation, foul smelling, or bloody droppings is a clear sign to seek veterinary assistance. Immediately consult the veterinarian and share the signs and symptoms you have noted for effective diagnosis and treatment.

Egg Laying Issues

When your duck stays too long in the nesting area, does not lay eggs regularly, and produces abnormal eggs, that indicates issues with the reproductive system. Taking it for a checkup by a certified veterinarian is the next step here.

Lameness or Mobility Issues

Injuries and certain medical conditions can cause ducks to experience issues with standing and walking and problems affecting their feet and legs. A professional veterinary evaluation is essential to accurately diagnose the problem and recommend appropriate treatments to improve their mobility and quality of life.

Injuries

Ducks can sustain injuries from various sources, and wounds, cuts, fractures, or conditions like bumblefoot (foot infections) can compromise their health. Seeking veterinary care for prompt and proper treatment is crucial to prevent infections, manage pain, and ensure optimal healing.

Parasite Infestations

Both internal and external parasites can adversely affect ducks' health. Suppose you observe signs of infestation, such as visible parasites on their skin or feathers, weight loss, weakness, or poor growth. In that case, it's essential to involve a veterinarian. Timely intervention can prevent parasites from causing further harm and discomfort to your ducks.

Sudden Deaths

Unexpected deaths within your flock should raise concern. While some deaths might occur naturally, sudden losses may indicate the presence of contagious diseases that could spread. Consulting a veterinarian can help you determine the cause and appropriate steps to prevent further losses.

Visible Symptoms

Any physical changes in ducks' appearance, such as swelling, discoloration, open sores, or abnormal growths, require professional evaluation. A veterinarian can accurately diagnose the condition, recommend treatments, and prevent potential complications.

Decreased Egg Production

A sudden drop in egg production or changes in egg quality, such as thin shells or unusual shapes, may signal reproductive issues. Seeking veterinary advice can help diagnose and address these problems to ensure the health of your ducks and their egg-laying capabilities.

Eye or Nasal Issues

Ducks with symptoms like eye discharge, swelling, redness, or nasal discharge may be experiencing eye or respiratory infections. Consulting a veterinarian is necessary to prevent further discomfort and complications.

Unexplained Weight Loss

Significant weight loss in ducks could indicate various health problems, including infections, parasites, or internal issues. Veterinary assistance is crucial for identifying the underlying cause and determining the best action.

Neurological Signs

Ducks displaying neurological symptoms like head tilting, tremors, seizures, or abnormal behavior require immediate veterinary evaluation. A professional assessment is necessary to determine the cause and provide appropriate care.

Changes in Vocalizations

Ducks communicate through vocalizations. If you notice one becoming unusually quiet or displaying new vocal patterns, it could indicate distress or illness. A veterinarian can assess the situation and recommend appropriate actions.

Flock-Wide Health Issues

If multiple ducks in your flock exhibit similar symptoms or a sudden decline in the overall health of your ducks, it may suggest a contagious disease. Veterinary consultation is essential to prevent disease spread and ensure proper treatment for affected ducks. Closely observing your ducks for behavior, appearance, or symptom changes is critical to their well-being. If you notice any concerning signs, seeking professional help from a veterinarian experienced in avian care is crucial for early diagnosis, effective treatment, and the long-term health of your duck flock.

Routine Checkups

Handling routine check-ups for your ducks requires careful planning, attentive observation, and a strong partnership with a skilled avian veterinarian. Regular veterinary visits are essential to monitor your ducks' health, identify emerging concerns, and ensure their well-being.

Here's a comprehensive guide on managing routine check-ups for your ducks:

- Begin by researching and establishing a relationship with a qualified avian veterinarian.
- Look for someone experienced in treating ducks or poultry, ideally located conveniently for regular visits.
- Contact the avian veterinarian to schedule routine check-up appointments for your ducks.
- Follow their recommended schedule, which may vary based on age, health history, and specific needs.
- Before the visit, compile a detailed record of your ducks' health history, including vaccinations, treatments, and previous health issues.
- Create a list of questions or concerns you'd like to discuss during the check-up.
- Make sure your ducks are comfortable and secure in a well-ventilated carrier or crate for transportation.

Discussing Things with the Veterinarian

During the check-up, allow the veterinarian to conduct a thorough physical examination of each duck. This involves assessing their weight, body condition, eyes, beak, feet, wings, and overall health. Take advantage of this time to share any observations or changes in behavior you've noticed since the last visit. Seek advice on diet, housing, disease prevention, and general care. The veterinarian may recommend diagnostic tests such as fecal exams, blood tests, or swabs to screen for potential health issues if necessary. Adhere to their recommendations for vaccinations, deworming, and other preventive measures tailored to your ducks' needs and potential disease risks.

The veterinarian will discuss potential treatment options, medications, and care instructions if they find any health issues. Make sure you understand the recommended treatment plan, including details about dosage, administration, and follow-up instructions. Don't hesitate to ask questions about duck care, behavior, diet, housing, or any other concerns you may have. Their expertise is a valuable resource. After the check-up, closely follow their guidance.

Chapter 7: The Beauty of the Duck Egg

Duck eggs aren't easy to crack because they have thicker shells than chicken eggs. Still, they should be handled with care. Collecting, maintaining, and storing duck eggs isn't a simple task. It takes time and effort, but it is worth it to keep them fresh so you can take advantage of their many health benefits.

Collecting, maintaining, and storing duck eggs isn't a simple task.
https://pixabay.com/photos/egg-duck-green-nest-nature-spring-4067035/

This chapter covers everything related to duck eggs. It will discuss their unique qualities, explain how to handle and take care of them, and provide simple and delicious recipes based on them.

Collecting and Handling Duck Eggs

Ducks lay eggs at night, so when you wake up the next day, they will be ready for you to collect. Let them out of their cages to exercise and forage while you look for the eggs.

Collect what you find right away; if you don't, they will nest with their eggs and stop producing. If you are raising them for eggs, you can't afford to go for days without new ones. So, schedule an hour every morning to go on a scavenger hunt in your ducks' coop.

Count the eggs first. If the number is low, this indicates that one or more of the ducks haven't yet produced any. They will most likely lay the eggs while they are outside. Keep an eye on them to spot where they lay. Usually, they choose the same spot every time, so this will make it easier to find them in the future.

Look for the eggs in their nesting boxes, housing area, and bedding. Check every corner because ducks can sometimes hide their eggs to protect them. This can take time and effort, but you'll soon familiarize yourself with their habits and learn their preferred locations.

The process of collecting the eggs is simple. You don't need any special equipment or even gloves. Simply remove the eggs with your hands, then place them in a small basket.

Tips for Handling Duck Eggs

- Wash your hands before and after you handle the eggs to protect the baby duckling from bacteria.

- Be careful when placing the eggs in the basket. Put them slowly and gently so they won't crack or break.

- Make sure the basket is made of solid materials so it won't break and damage the eggs.

Maintaining Egg Hygiene

While collecting the eggs is easy, the tricky part is cleaning them. Duck eggs are harder to clean than chicken eggs. They are usually covered with a gray layer that resembles a film and has an unpleasant odor.

Follow these steps to make the process easier for you.

Instructions:

1. After collecting the eggs, take the basket back home.
2. Using a clean, damp piece of cloth, wipe off the manure and mud.
3. Clean off the gray film with a kitchen scrubber.
4. Next, remove the bloom from the eggs by rinsing them in warm water, then clean them with a paper towel.

Some people prefer to leave the bloom because they believe it makes the eggs fresh for long periods and protects them from bacteria and air. Others claim that if you are going to sell your eggs or use them right away, you shouldn't worry about the shelf life. Consider the two opinions and choose what is best for you.

Eggs covered with blooms look unappetizing, so if shelf life isn't a concern, remove it. However, if you aren't going to sell the eggs and the bloom doesn't bother you, keep it. If you want to wash it, use warm water. Never wash the eggs with cold water, and avoid soaking them because they will get contaminated.

Storing Duck Eggs

After collecting and cleaning the eggs, you should properly store them to prevent spoilage, prolong their shelf life, and guarantee they will remain fresh for a long time.

Instructions:

1. Place them in an egg carton or container with the pointy end down to protect them from bacteria.
2. Label it with the date.
3. Store the carton in a cool place, preferably a refrigerator.
4. Place the eggs in the refrigerator to stabilize their temperature. If you store them on the door, their temperature will change every time you open it.
5. Use them for cooking, frying, or baking, just like chicken eggs.

Duck eggs will only last for three weeks at room temperature. Storing them in a refrigerator will give them a four-month shelf life. However, if you wash the eggs, they will only last for about five or six weeks in the fridge.

Duck eggs can easily go bad, but there is a simple test you can do to check if they are still fresh or not.

Instructions:

1. Fill a large glass jar or the kitchen sink with water.
2. Place one egg at a time in the water.
3. Fresh eggs will lay on their side or sink to the bottom.
4. Eggs that are starting to lose their freshness will sink but stand on one end. They are still safe but use them right away, preferably in baking.
5. Bad eggs will float. These aren't safe to use, so throw them away.

The Unique Qualities of Duck Eggs

There is a reason duck eggs are so popular, and more and more people prefer them over chicken eggs. They have unique qualities that set them apart, and they go beyond the delicious taste and nutritional benefits.

Long Shelf Life

Duck eggs have a longer shelf life than chicken eggs because they are larger, harder to crack, and have thicker membranes and shells. So they will remain fresh and delicious for long periods.

Creamier Taste

They contain high levels of proteins, vitamins, minerals, healthy fats, and more yolk than egg whites ratio. This gives them a much smoother, creamier, and richer taste than chicken eggs.

Large Size

They are noticeably larger than chicken eggs. It is then more economical to raise ducks for their eggs than chicken.

Great for Baking

Thanks to their high levels of proteins and fats, duck eggs are great for baking. They produce light cookies and bread that will melt in your mouth, high soufflés and meringues, and fluffier and more delicious cakes. They have the same culinary uses as chicken eggs, except they are tastier and creamier.

However, they can have a rubbery texture if you overcook them due to their low water content.

Contain More Nutrients

Ducks that are allowed to forage will produce eggs rich in nutrients. One egg can contain higher levels of iron, folate, choline, fatty acids, Omega-3, and Vitamins A and D than chicken eggs.

Different Types of Protein

Duck eggs contain a different type of protein than their counterpart. You can safely consume duck eggs if you are allergic to chicken eggs.

A More Eggy Taste

Duck eggs have a more eggy taste than any other bird. Although an egg's flavor mainly depends on the bird's diet, a duck's egg has a unique taste. Foraging feed plays a huge role here as well. Ducks that can eat whatever they want from nature produce eggs with a unique flavor.

More Expensive

If you plan to sell the eggs, you'll be happy to know that duck eggs are more expensive than chicken eggs. Since they are harder to find, have better and unique qualities, and are great for baking, many chefs and high-end restaurants favor them. You won't have any trouble selling them.

Now that you have learned about the many unique qualities of duck eggs, let's discover some simple and fun recipes to make creamy and delicious dishes!

Duck Egg Quiche with Seasonal Vegetables

This is a tasty dish you can eat for breakfast, brunch, lunch, or dinner. You can change the recipe and experiment with different types of vegetables.

Ingredients:

- 4 duck eggs
- 6 ounces of baby spinach
- 2 minced garlic cloves
- 1 homemade dough or pie crust
- 1 diced shallot
- 4 ounces of shredded cheddar cheese
- 1 cup of whole milk
- 1 teaspoon of sea salt
- 1 tablespoon of olive oil

Instructions:

1. Preheat your oven to 350°F.
2. Prepare the dough by rolling it out and placing it on a pie plate. If you are using store-bought pie crust, follow the instructions on the package.
3. Next, pour the olive oil into a large pan, place it on a stove, and heat it over medium-high heat.
4. Wait until it is hot, then add the shallots. Let them sauté for three minutes.
5. Then add the spinach and garlic and leave it to cook until the spinach wilts.
6. Pour the mixture into the base of the pie dough to form a layer.
7. Crack the duck eggs into a small bowl, then mix until the yolk breaks.
8. Add the salt, half the cheddar cheese, and milk to the eggs, then whisk to mix them together.
9. Pour the mixture over the spinach mixture, then spread the rest of the cheese.

10. Put the mixture in the oven and leave it to bake for fifty minutes.

11. Get it out of the oven and leave it to cool down for five minutes. Then slice and serve while it is still warm.

Classic Duck Egg Pasta Carbonara

This is a popular Italian dish that you can make for lunch.

Ingredients:

- 1 large, chopped bundle of parsley
- 1 large minced garlic clove
- 3 whisked duck egg yolks
- 200 grams of dried Linguine (a type of Italian pasta)
- 40 grams of grated Parmesan cheese
- 50 grams of diced smoked pancetta (type of pork)
- 100 grams of cubed smoked pancetta
- Pinch of pepper to taste
- Grated Parmesan (for serving)

Instructions:

1. Pour water into a large pot and add salt, then leave it to boil.

2. Put the dried linguine in the pot and leave it to cook for eleven minutes.

3. Prepare the sauce while the pasta is cooking.

4. Place a large empty frying pan over the stove and leave it over low heat.

5. Next, add the diced pancetta, then gradually increase the heat over a few minutes until the fats melt away from the pancetta and it turns crisp.

6. Remove the pancetta, but leave the fat in the pan.

7. Lower the heat to medium-high, add the cubed pancetta to the pan, and leave it to cook with the fat for three minutes.

8. Next, add the garlic to the pan and leave them to cook until the pancetta starts to crisp.

9. Remove the pan from the stove.

10. Take the linguine out of the pot and drain it. Don't discard the water.

11. Add the linguine to the pan, then splash some of the pasta water over it.

12. Spread the grated parmesan and the duck egg yolk over the pan.

13. Mix the yolk with the pancetta and linguine and leave them to gently cook.

14. Add more cooking pasta water to make the sauce glossy and loose.

15. Season with the parsley and black pepper.

16. Twist the pasta onto plates with a long fork, then sprinkle the crisp pancetta.

17. Sprinkle more grated parmesan, then serve while it's hot.

Duck Egg French Toast with Caramelized Apples

Enjoy this sweet treat for breakfast or brunch. Serve it hot.

Ingredients for Caramelized Apples:

- ½ teaspoon of cinnamon
- ½ cup of sugar
- ½ cup of water
- ¼ cup of butter
- 2 apples

Ingredients for French Toast:

- 2 duck eggs
- 4 slices of bread
- 2 tablespoons of frying butter
- 2 tablespoons of almond milk
- ½ teaspoon of cinnamon
- 2 tablespoons of granulated sugar

Instructions:

1. Peel the apples, then cut them into slices or cubes.

2. Put the apples in a pot, then add half a cup of sugar, water, and butter.

3. Leave it to cook over the stove for fifteen minutes and stir frequently to prevent it from sticking or burning.

4. Once the apples soften, remove them from the stove.

5. Break the duck eggs in a small bowl, then beat them together with a whisk.

6. Add the cinnamon, almond milk, and two tablespoons of sugar to the duck eggs, then whisk to mix together.

7. Dip each slice of the bread from both sides in the egg mix.

8. Heat a skillet over medium-high, then add the butter and let it melt.

9. Add the French toast and let it cook from both sides until it turns gold.

10. Put the caramelized apples over the French toast and serve hot.

Garlic and Chili Duck Egg Fried Rice

This Chinese dish is easy to make. You don't have to use the same ingredients in the recipe. You can experiment with different ones and get creative.

Ingredients:

- 2 lightly beaten duck eggs
- 3 tablespoons of peanut oil or duck fat
- 3 chopped cloves of garlic
- 2 tablespoons of soy sauce
- 2 peeled and diced carrots
- 3 chopped scallions (separate the green and white parts)
- 3 cups of cooled and cooked rice
- 1 to 3 chopped hot and small chilies
- 1 cup of fresh peas
- ½ pound of shredded duck meat, preferably leftover
- 1 tablespoon of sesame oil

Instructions:

1. Heat a large frying pan over the stove.

2. Next, add the peanut oil or duck fat and leave it to cook until it smokes.

3. Add the white part of the scallions, chilies, and garlic to the frying pan. Stir for thirty seconds.

4. Add the peas, carrots, rice, and duck meat, then stir for two minutes.

5. Push the ingredients to the side of the frying pan, then add the duck eggs.

6. Let it set while swirling with a chopstick.

7. Stir fry it into the rice and leave it for one minute. Don't touch it.

8. It should turn brown and crispy.

9. Next, pour the soy sauce over the rice edges, then mix.

10. Take it off the heat, then add the sesame oil.

Decadent Duck Egg Chocolate Mousse

This delicious chocolate mousse is creamy and tasty and can be the perfect dessert for you and your loved ones.

Ingredients:

- 3 large duck eggs
- 1 cup of cold and heavy cream
- 2 tablespoons of strong coffee
- 4 ½ ounces of chopped bittersweet chocolate
- 1 tablespoon of sugar
- 2 tablespoons of cubed and unsalted butter
- Whipped cream (optional)
- Raspberries (optional)

Instructions:

1. Whip the heavy cream until it softens, then let it chill.

2. Place the heavy coffee, butter, and chocolate in a double boiler over steamy, hot water. Stir until it turns smooth.

3. Remove the double boiler from the stove and leave it to cool or until the chocolate feels warm.

4. After the mixture cools, whip the egg whites until they turn creamy and form a shape.

5. Add the sugar, then whip again until the egg whites form stiff peaks.

6. Add the egg yolks, then stir.

7. Add ⅓ of the whipped cream to the chocolate mix and stir until it loosens.

8. Then add half the egg whites and stir.

9. Add the rest of the egg white, and sir.

10. Add the whipped cream, then stir.

11. Serve the mousse with a spoon in small dishes.

12. Add the whipped cream and raspberries on top for decoration, then leave them in the refrigerator for eight to twenty-four hours.

Smoked Salmon Eggs Benedict

If you love seafood, you'll enjoy this dish. This recipe is similar to eggs benedict with a couple of twists.

Eggs and Hollandaise Sauce Ingredients:

- 3 tablespoons of unsalted butter
- 1 sprig of fresh basil
- ¼ teaspoon of cardamom
- 1 sprig of fresh tarragon
- 2 coriander seeds
- 1 bay leaf
- 2 white peppercorns
- 1 minced shallot
- 1 minced garlic clove
- 4 duck egg yolks
- ⅓ cup of water

Smoked Salmon Topper Ingredients:
- Pinch of cayenne pepper
- 1 tablespoon of freshly squeezed lemon juice
- 1 tablespoon of mayonnaise
- ½ teaspoon of Dijon mustard
- 4-6 slices of smoked salmon
- 2 duck eggs
- White wine vinegar

Instructions:
1. Place the basil, cardamom, tarragon, coriander, bay leaf, peppercorns, shallot, and garlic in a small saucepan.
2. Leave it to boil on slow heat.
3. Reduce the heat to low, then let it simmer for ten minutes.
4. Strain with a sieve or cheesecloth, then set the liquid aside and discard the remaining ingredients.
5. Place the egg yolks in a double boiler.
6. Whisk until the yolks turn soft and fluffy.
7. Add the butter to the mixture while whisking.
8. Keep whisking until it thickens.
9. Remove the sauce from the stove, cover it with foil, and place it in a warm spot.
10. Put the duck eggs in boiling water and sprinkle some salt over it, then pour a splash of white wine vinegar.
11. Once they are cooked, remove the eggs from the water with a spoon.
12. Put the small salmon mixture over the poached duck eggs.
13. Pour the sauce over the dish.

Creamy Duck Egg Flan

This is a delicious dessert you can prepare and store in the fridge for two days and serve to your guests on a warm summer day.

Ingredients:

- 2 duck yolks
- 4 duck eggs
- 1 tablespoon of vanilla extract
- 1 can of condensed milk
- 1 ¼ cups of granulated sugar
- Pinch of salt

Instructions:

1. Preheat the oven to 350°F.
2. Place the vanilla extract, salt, condensed milk, and whipping cream in a saucepan.
3. Bring it to low or medium heat and stir frequently.
4. Remove the saucepan from the stove and let the mixture steep for fifteen minutes.
5. Next, get another saucepan and mix one cup of sugar with ⅓ of water.
6. Leave it on medium heat and stir until the sugar dissolves.
7. Reduce to low heat and let it simmer until the mixture thickens and caramelizes.
8. Pour the sugar mixture into custard cups.
9. Put on oven mitts and swirl the sides of the mixture in each cup.
10. Place the cups in a large baking pan.
11. Blend the egg yolks and whole eggs with the milk mixture.
12. Pour the mixture into the cups (divide them evenly).
13. Boil water and pour it into the baking pan.
14. Put it in the oven and let it bake for forty minutes.
15. Next, remove the pan from the oven and leave the cups to cool down.

Ducks lay eggs every day. Check your flock in the morning and collect them right away. Handle the eggs with care to avoid cracking them. Clean them from the mud using a damp or dry towel. Avoid washing them, or you'll shorten their shelf life. If you use them right away, you can wash them to remove the bloom since it is unsanitary.

Duck eggs are unique in more ways than one. They are large, delicious, creamy, and have a long shelf life. You can incorporate them in many recipes, and they can alter the flavor and texture of your dish. They also have many health benefits, and you can use them instead of chicken eggs in any recipe.

Chapter 8: Ethical Considerations and Best Practices

Raising ducks may not be as hip or profitable as chicken farming, but the practice is gradually on the rise. It has even become an emerging trend in many parts of the world.

Ducks, especially ducklings, are absolutely adorable. You can train them to a certain extent or simply play with them outdoors. Imprinted ducklings will stay with you throughout their lifespan. Duck eggs are larger and more nutritious than chicken eggs. Last but not least, these waterfowl are a great source of meat, too.

Ducks, especially ducklings, are absolutely adorable.
https://pixabay.com/photos/ducklings-pair-birds-beaks-animals-1853178/

If you have a passion for poultry farming, there is no reason why you should not raise ducks. Don't just jump on the bandwagon to gain acceptance or popularity by posting cute duckling pictures and videos on social media. There's nothing wrong with that, but it shouldn't be your only reason for raising these adorable animals.

Raise ducks for the right reasons, and more importantly, raise them the right way. To do that, you'll need to understand the moral ambiguities surrounding various techniques.

Ethical Considerations of Raising Ducks

Raising ducks as pets doesn't have any ethical conflicts, except one, and it's a big one. It's the universal argument against keeping all animals as pets. Here's how the logic goes. In a democracy, you choose to be under the president's authority. You have chosen that person to govern your country. They have your consent, and you have their consent to govern you.

Take an example closer to home. An employee works under their employer. They have chosen to work under the employer's authority. The employer has consented to let the employee work under them. There is mutual consent here.

In the case of animals or birds, you are the only one who consents to place them under your authority and make them your pet since the creature cannot communicate its consent. It may learn to love you over time, but while adopting or purchasing the being, it may hate you for taking away its freedom. You may like how it looks and behaves, but it doesn't know its feelings for you yet.

In the case of animals or birds, you are the only one who consents to place them under your authority and make them your pet since the creature cannot communicate its consent.

The situation is akin to a stalker kidnapping their prey. The kidnapped person may hate the stalker for taking their freedom. Over time, if they are treated well, they may begin to like their abductor. It's the harsh truth of keeping pets. You know that the animal or bird is better off with you, but it doesn't know that. It's the way of life, the survival of the fittest. Chalk it up to the greater good and move on.

Alternatively, are you planning to raise ducks only for practical purposes, like the production of eggs and meat? Your apprehension about becoming too attached to them is perfectly understandable. It doesn't mean that you should entirely ignore caring for them. Did you know that healthy, well-cared ducks give better eggs and meat? Either way, there are a few ethical considerations (don'ts) you need to consider.

• Don't Keep a Duck without Company

Dogs and cats may thrive with your company alone. Ducks, however, can rarely survive without fellow ducks or ducklings. Even if they do, they will remain troubled throughout their lifespan and die a miserable death. Just like humans, they feel loneliness and sorrow. They need to socialize, procreate, and communicate.

• Don't Keep a Duck in Your House

Just like most other birds, ducks value their freedom. They may not fly much, but they love swimming and roaming around under the open sky. If you keep your ducks in the house, they will eventually become overwhelmed with negative emotions, and they may lash out by making a lot of noise or even getting violent.

• Don't Let Them Roam Free All the Time

Ducks require proper care, and ducklings are even more so. They have a lot, from the bold crows to the ferocious bobcats. If you let them roam free in your neighborhood, a hawk may swoop in and carry away the ducks, or a raccoon may steal the ducklings. Be sure to build a secure coop for them to play in or keep your backyard door shut.

• Don't Keep Ducks Away from Water

Ducks are called waterfowl for good reason. They bathe and play in water. They require water to clean their feathers and to clear their eyes and nostrils free of dirt. Additionally, they love to splash around in a pool, swim for long hours, and submerge their heads to clean their entire body.

• Choose the Breed According to Your Requirements

Different breeds of ducks specialize in different actions. For instance, Khaki Campbell ducks produce the maximum number of eggs among all other breeds. On the other hand, the White Pekin is best known for its meat quality. If you want a pet duck, you may consider a Magpie. It's easy on the eye and rarely has any problems - a perfect beginner's duck.

• Don't Raise Ducks Just to Try Out Poultry Farming

Ducks aren't ideal for beginning your poultry farming venture. Try chickens or dogs if you are new to animal and bird care. Ducks are primarily for experienced caretakers. The big reason is their lifespan. Ducks can live for nearly 20 years.

Down the road, if you don't wish to care for them anymore, you can't just leave them in the wild and hope they survive. They probably won't survive a week in the wild.

While abandoning any animals or birds under your care is cruel, duck desertion is especially heartless. Admittedly, they can survive in a flock, as you may have read in a previous chapter. Domesticated ducks have an entirely different disposition. They may be less careful and more prone to being attacked by predators.

Now that you know what you should not do while raising ducks, here's what you can do while adhering to the ethics of the entire process.

Best Practices of Raising Ducks

So far, you learned the basic and advanced techniques of raising ducks. It's time to take a look at everything you can do to get the best out of this. The best practices vary depending on your reasons for raising ducks.

Raising Ducklings

Ducks need a lot of care, and ducklings need even more. Since they are lovable little creatures, you won't feel the burden of your chores one bit.

- **Feeding:** Ducklings need to be given food different from ducks only for the first two or three weeks of their life. You must ensure that their feed is high in protein (at least 20%). You also need to give them a decent amount (around 0.45 mg per 500 grams body weight) of niacin (vitamin B-3) per day. Niacin deficiency may cause serious problems, ranging from lameness to body deformities.

- **Watering:** Did you know that your duckling's health will begin to deteriorate within just a few hours without water? They require water after waking up, before and after eating, before playing, while playing, after playing, and before going to sleep. You get the gist!

On average, a baby duck will consume half a gallon of water each week, which doesn't seem much. That's because they also tend to splash around in the water, spilling most of it out. It is ideal to have a water fountain to pump clean water from time to time. But if you are using a tub or a bucket, make sure to refill it with clean water every few hours.

- **Swimming:** Typically, ducklings can learn to swim soon after hatching. The problem lies in their ability to fend off the cold. Adult ducks don't catch the chill after swimming because they secrete a layer of waterproofing oil on their feathers. Ducklings need around four to five weeks to start producing that oil and protect themselves from the cold.

  You can place your ducklings in the water earlier than four weeks, but ensure they don't stay in too long. As soon as they are out of the water, keep a heat lamp over them or place them in a brooder so they won't become cold.

- **Brooding:** Ducklings can be brooded in any type of brooding house, but it's best done in a nest. You may use a heat lamp or a warming plate. Keep it well-ventilated with a constant supply of water. They only need enough space to move around a bit, so don't make the nest too big. Set the temperature to about 85 degrees F, and you may reduce it by around 5-6 degrees each week. They only need to brood for the first two to four weeks after hatching.

- **Bedding:** Ducklings are most comfortable in a bed made of straw, which is also moisture-absorbent. Since ducklings make a lot of mess, you'll need to change the bedding often, and straw is easy to find and replace. The shorter the stems, the more at ease the ducklings will be. Other bedding alternatives include old hay, pine shavings, or mulch.

Raising Ducks for Meat

Ducks are usually ready to be butchered for meat after 7-8 weeks, which is why they cannot be raised like pet ducks.

- **Breeds/Species:** Not all breeds of ducks are ideal for meat. A few breeds aren't to everyone's taste, like the shoveler duck. On the other hand, a few others are perfect for human consumption. If you are thinking of raising an assortment of meat ducks, consider starting with a Pekin or a Muscovy. You can later progress to a Moulard or a Rouen.

- **Feeding:** Since you'll be using the ducks for meat as soon as they are ready, you'll need to feed them a diet very high in protein. The recommended proportion is 25% in the early stages while gradually bringing it down to around 20% in the 7th or 8th week.

- **Watering:** Keep a constant source of drinking water in the vicinity, like a duck fountain. Make sure that it's clean at all times because you'll be consuming what they are drinking. Mature ducks will need more water than ducklings (roughly 0.20 to 0.50 gallons).

- **Swimming:** Ducks don't need to swim, but they will be happier if they can at least once a day. Put up a shallow fountain or bowl for ducklings so that they don't drown. Once they mature and can float around for hours, let them play in a deeper and wider pool.

- **Brooding:** Since your eight-week-old ducks won't be producing eggs, their brooding house should be constructed like that of ducklings. Maintain a temperature of around 80F.

- **Bedding:** You don't need to switch your duckling's bedding when they mature into a duck. If you have been using straw so far, then stick with straw. They have gotten used to it underneath them while sleeping. If you change the material to hay in the middle of their growth, they may start feeling uncomfortable.

Raising Ducks for Eggs

If you are raising ducks only for consuming or selling eggs, then it's not a feasible option. The costs of nurturing ducks will be much higher than the eggs purchased at a supermarket. You may also want to consider raising them for meat or just keeping them as pets.

Hens generally start laying eggs when they are six to seven months old. They may keep producing a relatively high quantity of eggs until around eight years of age, after which their egg-laying capacity gradually begins to decline, completely stopping around two years later. If you are raising them for meat as well, it is recommended that you slaughter them when they are 18 months old.

- **Breeds/Species:** While all female ducks lay eggs, the number of eggs laid per year varies from species to species. The Khaki Campbell is preferred by most duck egg lovers in the world. It lays around 300 eggs per year and is also one of the easiest breeds to take care of. Runner ducks, primarily from Malaysia, also can reach the 300 mark. For a decent range of around 200-250 eggs per year, you may consider raising Magpie, Saxony, Pekin, Ancona, or Welsh Harlequin.

- **Feeding:** When they are in the duckling stage, they will need around 20% protein and a decent amount of niacin. Their (both ducklings and ducks) feed should be especially rich in calcium (around 4%) to ensure strong eggs. Most duck feeds available in the market contain the right proportion of nutrients, but it doesn't hurt to check before buying.

- **Watering:** As with ducklings and meat ducks, egg layers also need a lot of water to produce good-quality eggs. Keep a flowing fountain near their home, often refreshed with clean water. A pond will require you to clean the water soon after they drink it.

- **Swimming:** Egg layers swim the same amount of time as meat ducks, so be sure to construct an outdoor pool.

- **Brooding:** Different breeds of ducks brood for different time periods. The Khaki Campbell requires at least three weeks of brooding, whereas the Pekin may be done within two weeks. The brooding house should be the same as that mentioned for ducklings. Remember, moisture, ventilation, and heat are key to ensure successful brooding of ducks.

- **Bedding:** Ducks need ventilation as much as they require protection from predators. Their coop needs to have many windows and a roof to keep flying carnivores at bay. You don't need to create special bedding for adult ducks. They will forage the necessary materials and build a nest on their own. To help them out, you may just place a pile of straw or a bale of old hay nearby.

Raising Ducks as Pets or Ornaments

Do you wish to show off your ducks to your friends and neighbors or on social media? Try raising breeds that are known for their beauty. Ornamental ducks aren't usually known for the taste of their meat, and their eggs are simply an added bonus (they may produce around 100-200 eggs per year). With pet ducks, your primary focus should be on their health.

With pet ducks, your main focus should be on their health.
https://www.pexels.com/photo/selective-focus-photo-of-flock-of-ducklings-perching-on-gray-concrete-pavement-1300355/

- **Breeds/Species:** You need to be very careful while choosing the breed of your pets. All ducklings look adorable, but the question is how they appear as grownups. Do you want to add a splash of color to your coop? Go for the Mallard, Cayuga, and Wood duck breeds. Do you wish to create a sober atmosphere? You can never go wrong with Rouen or Buff Orpington ducks.

- **Feeding:** Feeding your ducklings is the same as mentioned in a previous section. Once it grows into an adult, you can let it forage for food on its own. They will eat insects, bugs, earthworms, and even certain plant leaves and roots. For proper nutrition and safety from predators, always keep their feed bowl filled so they won't have to venture out into the wild.

- **Watering:** The water requirements of pet and ornamental ducks are the same as all other breeds (0.25 to 0.50 gallons per day).

- **Swimming:** They need to swim often – like all other duck breeds – so build a sufficiently large pool within reach.

- **Brooding:** Egg layers, even if they lay fewer eggs than other species, need to brood for a set number of weeks. Their brooding coop need be no different than that of other breeds.

- **Bedding**: Straw is the most commonly used bedding for pet ducks, just like their meat and egg-laying counterparts.

Home Duck Slaughtering Tips

As you know by now, most meat ducks are ready to be butchered after about 7 weeks. Nevertheless, it is prudent to wait for a few months before slaughtering them so that you can get more meat out of them. Wait times differ for different species. For instance, Muscovy ducks grow to the ideal weight of six pounds in about four months, whereas you can get a 10-pound Pekin within just two months. Once they are ready, heed the following tips to get optimum meat from your ducks.

- Don't feed the ducks for around 14 hours before butchering to make the process easier.

- Killing a duck with a killing cone is easier and more humane, but if you can't find a large enough cone, you may consider hanging it with a rope tied to its legs and then killing it.

- The actual process of butchering starts with either skinning or plucking. Make sure that the butcher knife is sharp while skinning. Before plucking, you need to scald the duck in a pot of heated water. Then, simply pluck it by hand.

- Set your butchering station under a tap or near a lake to ensure a quick, easy clean.

- Place the butchered meat in the fridge for 24 hours before transferring it to the freezer.

Humane Duck Killing

- Place the duck upside down in the killing cone. This inverted posture will make its final moments more peaceful and relaxing.

- Grab its head by the beak and slice your knife slightly above its jawline. That's where its main artery is located. It won't feel the pain at all as it quickly bleeds out.

Chapter 9: Integration, Companionship, and Breeding

Much like humans have complex societal structures and norms, ducks have their ways of establishing order. To raise ducks, it is necessary to understand their social order so that you can meet them on their level. Recognizing that different environments will impact your birds in varying ways is the beginning of understanding duck behavior. You have to meet in the middle by interpreting their body language and behavioral responses. Observing your ducks can reveal details about their desires and needs.

Attention to detail is key for compassionately raising these interesting birds. Much like humans, they can be cryptic and difficult to understand if you are uninformed. Just like you must observe tone and body language to fully grasp what a person is communicating, for ducks, you can interpret their mood, mindset, and personality by the specifics of how they engage with you and your other animals. Through this subtle communication, you'll find out how unique each duck is based on their temperaments and interactions with you. The duck kingdom is full of characters, so we are in for a turbulent but fun journey. Do not let the little humps throw you off course. When it comes to these animals, perseverance is key.

Ducks wear their hearts on their wings. If you know what to look for, you'll immediately know when they are unhappy. Ducks demonstrate complex interpersonal interactions, from their bonds with caregivers to their socialization within groups. Understanding these behaviors can help you breed ducks and create a home that maximizes their well-being. Respect and patience are the pillars that hold up successful duck rearing. Making decisions with the best interests of your ducks in mind will result in a happy and healthy flock.

Depending on your desired outcomes, you must make a duck habitat that supports the goals you envision for your flock. Caring for ducks is approached differently if you are raising ducks for produce or keeping them as pets. Ducks can be aggressive, and they often bite people. To prevent injury to your birds or people they encounter, you must be aware of the warning signs of aggression and what is most conducive to a calm environment. In essence, if you play nice, your ducks will play nice. You just need to understand that they perceive the world differently from you, so communication requires a shift in perspective.

Meeting at the point of interspecies understanding is where the magic of duck-raising manifests. Once you learn to decode the sounds and actions of your ducks, you'll be given insight into their world. Furthermore, you'll open a doorway for your animals to connect with you. Ethical duck raising requires creating an environment that allows your ducks to be comfortable, calm, and content. As social creatures, ducks will form a relationship with you as a caregiver and with other members of your flock. You must facilitate desirable behavior because small mistakes can charge up aggressively intolerable ducks.

Social Interactions of Ducks

Ducks function within large social groups. It is possible to raise a solitary duck, but they will form bonds with you. Groups of ducks are called *paddlings*. Wild ducks migrate to follow favorable weather patterns, but domestic ducks typically stay in the area where they were raised. These dangerous migrations are part of the reason why ducks have formed such complex social structures. In nature, for ducks to survive, cooperation means the difference between paddling gracefully around a scenic pond or becoming a midday snack.

Ducks function within large social groups.
https://pixabay.com/photos/ducks-chicks-mallards-birds-7251870/

Ducks have evolved a linear social hierarchy known as a pecking order, especially when it comes to mating. The female ducks lay eggs according to who is the highest ranking. The lead gets to lay eggs first, with the other ducks following in descending order of importance. Male ducks, or drakes, also have a similar order, with the male lead getting to mate first. The hens guard their eggs as a collective. The pecking order also applies to feeding, with the lead ducks eating first and lower-ranking ducks eating last.

All breeds are not created equal. Some are docile, while others are more aggressive. You need to think about this before deciding which ducks you'll breed. Breeds like the Pekin duck guard their nests more aggressively, often resulting in conflict with people or other animals. When choosing a breed to raise, it is essential to weigh the dynamics of your property. If you have dogs, you may want to get a less aggressive breed because an altercation between a dog and a duck can have bloody consequences. Ducks will attack small children if they feel that their nests are being threatened, so if you have young ones running around, they need to be educated about how to behave around ducks. Preferably, you can choose a breed that is more well-suited for kids to interact with.

One way to reduce aggression is by separating the hens from the drakes. Both hens and drakes can be protective of their mating partners, which means keeping a mix of the two sexes doesn't often end well, especially among more aggressive breeds. Space can also become an issue because the evolutionary biology of ducks is catered to traveling long distances and moving around a lot. Therefore, keeping ducks inside your home is not advised because it can create distress for those who prefer spaciousness.

Bonding with Caregivers

The social inclinations of ducks make it easier to establish bonds with them. Unlike other bird species that are solitary and unable to care for you, ducks are sentimental beings. One of the key occurrences that highlight the social nature of ducks is the phenomenon of imprinting. When a duckling hatches in the wild, it will imprint on its mother and a few of its siblings. Imprinting is an attachment that is formed, which helps a duckling determine who it should follow. If you are the primary caregiver for a duckling, it will imprint on you, especially if no other ducks are around.

If a duck imprints on you, it will identify humans as part of its social circle for as long as it lives. This could help in an environment where ducks often interact with people. Wildlife specialists have warned against leading wild ducks to imprint on humans because it puts them at a disadvantage in the natural world. For domestic animals, imprinting is not an issue. Ducks that have imprinted on humans will not necessarily be socialized and friendly. The imprinting process means that ducks will not fear humans, which could have the adverse impact of leading to aggressive behavior.

Allowing your ducks to imprint on you is not advisable, even though it sounds like a great experience. Imprinted ducks are a far cry from the picturesque imagery of a princess dancing along a forest pathway with tame animals following as she sings high notes. Ducks that have imprinted on humans are at a disadvantage because they get stuck in a weird limbo of being unable to fully socialize with ducks or humans. Therefore, ducklings should spend most of their time with their mother to be fully socialized into the duck community. Caring for your ducklings is important at the early, vulnerable stage of their lives, but it cannot be done by sacrificing their long-term wellness.

Wild ducks that have imprinted on humans can never be released back into their natural habitats. Therefore, if your ducks have imprinted on you, it is a lifetime commitment. Domesticated ducks spend their entire lives on a farm or homestead, so human imprinting in that context is not as detrimental. Ducks are genetically wired to form strong relationships within their support system. Since you'll be raising ducks, you are now integrated into their social circle.

How to Introduce New Ducks to an Existing Flock

Since ducks can be confrontational, introducing new ones into your flock must be well-thought-out and planned. You cannot just dump a new duck in the pond and hope that everyone gets along. Just as humans have formalities and reservations about meeting new people, ducks must follow similar social protocols. First and foremost, before your new duck can get introduced to your flock, you must conduct a health evaluation. Ducks are resilient, but they can still fall ill. The medical evaluation of your new duck must include checks for respiratory illness, mobility issues, and parasites. Ducks are social and interact with one another in close proximity, so any infectious illness has the perfect mix of variables to spread quickly. During the period of medical evaluation, your new ducks should be quarantined.

The time you introduce new ducks is also important. The mating season of ducks is in the springtime. That is a terrible time to bring in new members. Hormones are going insane, so erratic behavior is almost guaranteed. Overzealous males can also hurt new females that are introduced into the flock.

Furthermore, females can also be competitive at this time due to their hormones, so this could lead to confrontations with a new hen. If you acquire new ducks during the mating season, it would be best to keep them separated until the season is over. The springtime can be volatile for ducks, so throwing someone new into the mix could be stirring the pot a little too much.

If you are tending multiple flocks, you can introduce the new duck to the group that you feel will be more welcoming. You could observe the interactions of your ducks daily so you can gauge which of your flocks are calmer. If a flock is already chaotic, it may be ill-advised to attempt to bring in any new ducks because that energy will get directed toward the newcomer. It will be easier if the flock that a new duck is introduced to is already docile and submissive. This submissive flock that you'll have the most ease with during introductions.

Any new ducks you wish to integrate must gradually be introduced to the flock. One method you can use is keeping the new duck separated but in an adjacent place where the ducks can interact without direct physical contact. This can give your flock time to adjust to the new member. Springing a sudden change can be jarring, so giving your ducks time to settle into the change is only fair. Remember that ducks form strong social bonds, so they have not yet connected with the new duck, who is an outsider. During this early integration period, you should closely monitor your ducks to make sure that nobody gets hurt.

Some fighting will occur at the initial stages of bringing a new duck into the flock. This conflict is normal because the group's social order must be established. The fighting is the ducks' way of organizing themselves into a neat hierarchy. Your observation will just be to ensure the fights do not get out of hand because you wouldn't want any of your ducks seriously injured. Feeding can be another issue when introducing new ducks. Observe how well your new ducks are eating because it is common for an original flock to shun new members from feeding areas. However, a new duck can be fully integrated into the flock after a couple of weeks with your help and guidance.

Mating Behaviors

The mating season is an interesting time for ducks. Just like human relationships, the love life of ducks can get complicated and competitive. Ducks communicate their mating intentions with body language. Their courting rituals include a lot of flirting. Males attract females with elaborate dance displays where they bob their heads and show off their feathers. An interested female will bob her head along with the male duck in an elaborate courting exercise.

Ducks' courting rituals include a lot of flirting.
https://pixabay.com/photos/rubber-ducks-wedding-wedding-couple-2402752/

Males will spread their wings and lift up their tails to show off their colorful secondary feathers to attract a female. The male will then submerge itself in water and pop back up, letting out a grunting whistle. This display is often done in groups so that a female can get her pick of the best suitor. Ducks use a variety of vocalizations and body language to communicate their intentions and feelings. Hissing is a sign of aggression, while other variations of quacks and honks communicate that they are happy or upset. These vocalizations can be used to collaborate, like when ducks fly together in formation.

Females who are interested in courtship will hold their heads low close to the water while swimming short distances. They will also bop their heads up and down to show their desire. Competition can become fierce since every female and male is trying to get the best conduit for their genetics. In the mating season, ducks will fight more and will be extra aggressive. Be aware that ducks may hurt you and your other animals in the mating season if you are not careful. Pay attention to their body language and vocalizations because they often provide warnings before they attack. A good habit to adopt during mating season is checking your ducks for injuries because of the increased risk of fighting during this period.

Ducks are semi-monogamous. Unlike some other bird species, like penguins that mate for life, ducks choose a new mate every season. The evolutionary advantage of this is the ability to choose the most suitable mates each year because they may have deteriorated over time. If you aim to breed your ducks, you must maintain an equal hen-to-drake ratio. This will minimize conflict and help you maintain a constant flow of new ducks by maximizing your breeding capabilities.

Nesting and Incubation

Ducks construct minimalistic nests on the ground made from twigs, reeds, and grass. If you want to harvest eggs, you should create a space with the appropriate requirements that a hen can use to construct a nest. Duck nests on the ground explain why they become protective after laying eggs. A nest on the ground is easily accessible to predators and can be trampled by mistake. To find nests, you should check reedy areas that are close to the water. Ducks are emotional and intelligent, so you should be careful and respectful when handling their nests or eggs. Approach the process of harvesting eggs with the utmost care.

As a breeder, you may want to ensure that all your eggs hatch. Therefore, you could incubate the eggs. Duck eggs take about 28 days to hatch inside an incubator. The humidity and temperature are important at this phase because slight changes can throw off this sensitive biological process. The humidity in the incubator should be set at 44% to 55% for the first 25 days. In the last three days, you can increase the humidity up to 65%. Your eggs should be turned at 180 degrees five times a day. You must be careful not to disturb the eggs too much. There is a pinpoint balance that must be reached with duck incubation. Some more sophisticated incubators turn the eggs automatically.

Raising Ducklings

Like any other young animal, ducklings require additional care. Your ducklings will be predominantly raised by their mother, or you'll hand-raise them in a brooder. If you are raising your ducklings without a hen, you are responsible for providing what the hen would have given the ducks, including food, warmth, shelter, and safety. The brooder in which your ducks are being raised must be soft and comfortable.

Temperature control is essential for raising healthy ducklings. The environment they live in should be 90 degrees. After a few days, you'll drop the temperature down to 85 degrees. You can then decrease the temperature by five degrees every week after that until they reach about thirty days old. It takes about three months for a duckling to grow fully. Heating is done with a lamp. If you see that your ducklings are huddling close together underneath the lamp, it means that they are getting cold. If your ducklings are panting and avoiding the lamp, they are getting too hot.

Ducklings swim from day one. You can start them off in a small container or even a bathtub before introducing them to a bigger body of water. They spend a large section of their time in the water. Ensuring your ducklings are happily swimming along is an exercise they will truly appreciate. The bigger your ducklings get, the more time they can spend outside in the sun and fresh air. Predators like cats, snakes, and birds are dangerous to your ducklings. As a mother will protect her brood, you must also keep a sharp eye out when the ducklings are in the yard. The bright yellow color of the feathers will slowly begin changing as they grow and is an indicator of maturity. They also have a specialized feed that you can get from qualified dealers, but they can also eat mealworms, chopped-up melon, and cooked oatmeal. Finally, ensure that your ducklings have a constant supply of drinking water in a small container.

Chapter 10: Challenges, Solutions and FAQs

Raising ducks becomes a breeze when you know the challenges that come with them. Maintaining the right approach and implementing adequate solutions will make your duck-raising journey enjoyable and hassle-free. Here's a quick refresher on the most common health issues and challenges.

Raising ducks might come with its set of challenges, but it is worth it.
https://www.pexels.com/photo/duckling-on-black-soil-during-daytime-162140/

Challenges in Duck Raising

Health Issues

Water Quality: Ducks are highly dependent on water. Make sure to provide them with clean, fresh water at all times. Stagnant or dirty water can lead to health problems, so change it regularly. Additionally, ducks should have access to a shallow pool to swim and clean themselves.

Parasites: Regularly inspect your ducks for external parasites like mites and lice. These can cause discomfort and various health issues. Consult a veterinarian to determine suitable treatments and preventive measures to keep your ducks parasite-free.

Respiratory Issues: Ducks develop respiratory illnesses, especially in humid and unsanitary living environments. Maintaining adequate ventilation and cleanliness can significantly prevent the growth of harmful bacteria or toxic gases like ammonia.

Botulism: Ducks are susceptible to botulism, a potentially fatal illness caused by toxins produced by bacteria in contaminated water. Keep their living area clean and remove any potential sources of contamination. Do not feed them spoiled or moldy food.

Aggressive Behavior

Socialization: Ducks have a pecking order and can exhibit aggression, especially when introducing new members to the flock. Gradually introduce new ducks, allowing them time to establish their hierarchy. Monitor their interactions and provide hiding spots to reduce stress.

Space: Overcrowding can lead to aggression. Make sure your ducks have enough space in their living area to move around comfortably. A lack of space can also contribute to stress and health problems.

Hiding Spots: Ducks need places to hide or escape. Provide hiding spots like boxes or bushes in their enclosure to allow them to retreat if they need to.

Dietary Concerns

Balanced Diet: Ducks require a balanced diet that includes waterfowl pellets, grains, and vegetables. Avoid relying solely on bread or unhealthy treats, as this can lead to nutritional imbalances.

Grit: Ducks need access to grit, such as small stones, to aid in digestion. Grit helps grind down food in their gizzard, improving their overall digestion.

Nutritional Supplements: Consult a veterinarian to determine if your ducks need additional vitamins or minerals, especially during stages like egg laying. A proper diet is crucial for their overall health and egg production.

Egg Laying Issues

Nesting Boxes: Provide comfortable and secure nesting boxes with clean bedding for your ducks to lay their eggs. A conducive nesting area reduces stress and encourages consistent egg-laying.

Egg Eating: Collect eggs frequently to prevent ducks from pecking and breaking them. Provide clean and comfortable nesting boxes to discourage egg-eating behavior.

Feeding Considerations

Adjustment: Modify the amount of food based on your ducks' age, size, and activity level. Avoid overfeeding, which can lead to obesity and related health issues.

Molting

Nutrition: During molting, ducks require extra nutrients for healthy feather regrowth. Make sure they receive a nutrient-rich diet to support this natural process.

Temperature Regulation

Hot Weather: Ducks can struggle in hot weather. Provide shade, cool water, and proper ventilation to help them stay comfortable. Avoid heat stress by monitoring their behavior.

Cold Weather: Ducks are more susceptible to cold in wet conditions. Insulate their shelter and provide adequate bedding to keep them warm during colder months.

Foot and Leg Health

Clean Bedding: Provide clean bedding to prevent foot infections. Regularly inspect your ducks' feet for cuts, sores, or signs of bumblefoot, which is a bacterial infection.

Social Dynamics

Observation: Watch for signs of bullying or isolation within the flock. If necessary, separate aggressive ducks to prevent stress and injuries.

Quarantine

New Ducks: Quarantine new ducks before introducing them to your existing flock. This prevents the potential spread of diseases.

Hygiene Practices

Cleanliness: Wash your hands after handling ducks or cleaning their environment to prevent the transmission of germs. Regularly disinfect equipment and tools you use for their care.

Routine Health Checks

Observation: Establish a routine for observing your ducks' overall health. Look for any changes in behavior, appetite, or physical condition that could indicate a health issue.

Interaction and Enrichment

Bonding: Spend time interacting with your ducks to build trust and strengthen your bond. Hand-feeding treats or simply spending time nearby can foster a positive relationship.

Enrichment: Provide environmental enrichment such as toys, shallow pools, and hiding spots to keep your ducks mentally stimulated and engaged.

Frequently Asked Questions

Egg Care

Q: How can you prevent egg eating in ducks?

A: To do that, provide clean and comfortable nesting boxes with sufficient bedding. Collect eggs promptly and consider using fake ones to discourage pecking.

Egg eating can become a habit if not addressed promptly. Ducks may accidentally break an egg and then learn to eat the contents. To prevent this behavior, create inviting nesting boxes with clean straw or bedding where ducks feel secure laying eggs. Collecting eggs frequently reduces the opportunity for ducks to peck at and consume them. Using fake eggs or golf balls in the nests can deter pecking behavior by providing an unappetizing experience.

Integrating Ducks

Q: How can you integrate new ducks into an existing flock?

A: Gradually introducing new ducks helps reduce stress and aggression. Initially, keep the new ducks separated but within sight of the existing flock initially. After a period of observation, allow supervised interactions to establish a pecking order. Provide hiding spots and multiple feeding stations to reduce competition and bullying.

Integrating new ducks into an existing flock requires a thoughtful approach to minimize stress and potential conflicts. Ducks are social animals but establish a pecking order that can lead to initial tensions. By allowing the new ducks to see and hear the existing flock before direct contact, you reduce the shock of introduction. Supervised interactions in a neutral space allow ducks to establish their hierarchy without severe aggression. Providing hiding spots and multiple food and water sources ensures that new and existing ducks have enough resources, reducing the risk of bullying and promoting a smoother integration process.

Winter Care

Q: How do you keep ducks warm in winter?

A: Insulate the duck shelter using straw, hay, or other suitable materials to provide warmth. Ensure proper ventilation to prevent moisture buildup, which can lead to frostbite. Ducks generate body heat, so huddling together can help keep them warm. Provide ample bedding, offer access to clean, unfrozen water, and protect them from drafts.

Ducks are more cold-hardy than they might appear, but providing appropriate winter care is important for their comfort and health. Insulating their shelter with materials like straw or hay traps heat and creates a warmer environment. Adequate ventilation prevents excessive humidity and moisture buildup, which can lead to frostbite and respiratory issues. Ducks tend to huddle together for warmth, so provide enough space and bedding for them to do so comfortably. Offering access to clean and unfrozen water is crucial for hydration and overall well-being. Preventing drafts and providing a snug and insulated shelter contribute to your ducks' ability to withstand colder temperatures.

Vaccinations

Q: Do ducks need vaccinations?

A: While ducks typically don't require routine vaccinations, consult a poultry veterinarian for recommendations based on your specific location and circumstances. Vaccinations can vary by region and disease prevalence.

The need for vaccinations in ducks varies depending on factors such as your region and the prevalence of specific diseases. Ducks are generally resilient birds, but certain diseases can impact their health and egg production. Consulting a poultry veterinarian with knowledge of local disease risks can determine if vaccinations are necessary to protect your ducks. Regular veterinary care, proper nutrition, and a clean living environment are key components of maintaining the health and well-being of your ducks.

Sexing Ducks

Q: How can you tell if your ducks are male or female?

A: Sexing ducks can be challenging, especially in some breeds. While males (drakes) often have curled tail feathers and females (ducks) have a more subtle quack, accurate sex determination might require professional expertise or DNA testing.

Sexing ducks can be difficult, especially when they're young. In some breeds, males and females have distinct visual differences, such as curled tail feathers in males and a more subdued quack in females. However, these indicators might not be foolproof, and variations can occur. Professional expertise or DNA testing is often the most accurate way to determine the sex of ducks. Some physical and behavioral differences may become more apparent as ducks mature, but relying solely on visual cues can lead to misidentifications.

Broody Ducks

Q: What do you do if your duck becomes broody?

A: Broodiness is a natural behavior where ducks sit on eggs to hatch them. If you're not interested in hatching eggs, gently discourage this behavior by promptly removing eggs. You can also offer distractions and consider isolating the broody duck for a short time.

Broodiness is an instinctual behavior where ducks want to incubate and hatch eggs. While this behavior is natural, it may not always be convenient if you're not interested in raising ducklings. To discourage broodiness, remove eggs from the nest as soon as possible. This prevents the duck from becoming too attached to the eggs and decreases the likelihood of successful incubation. Offering distractions like changing the nest location or providing new bedding can also break the broody cycle. If needed, you can isolate the broody duck in a separate area for a few days to redirect her focus.

Egg Laying

Q: When do ducks start laying eggs?

A: Ducks typically start laying eggs around 5-7 months of age, but this can vary based on factors such as breed, environmental conditions, and nutrition.

The age at which ducks start laying eggs depends on multiple factors. Most will begin laying between 5 and 7 months old, but this can vary widely based on breed and individual differences. Providing appropriate nutrition and ensuring a stress-free environment can encourage earlier and more consistent egg laying. Factors such as daylight duration and temperature can also influence egg production. By monitoring their behavior and providing proper care, you can ensure your ducks have a successful egg-laying season.

Duckling Care

Q: How do you care for ducklings?

A: Ducklings require a warm and safe environment. Use a brooder with a heat lamp to maintain the right temperature. Provide waters that are shallow and accessible for them to drink and clean themselves. Feed them a starter diet formulated specifically for ducklings.

Ducklings are delicate and require attentive care during their early stages of life. A brooder provides a controlled environment where temperature is crucial. A heat lamp or heating pad ensures that ducklings stay warm, as they cannot regulate their body temperature effectively. Shallow waters prevent accidental drowning. Ducklings need access to clean water for drinking and cleaning themselves. Starter diets for ducklings are specially formulated to provide the necessary nutrients for growth and development. Their nutritional requirements will change as they mature, so it's important to adjust their diet accordingly. Proper care and nutrition during the duckling stage set the foundation for healthy growth and adulthood.

Egg Incubation

Q: Can you incubate duck eggs without a mother duck?

A: Yes, you can incubate duck eggs artificially using an incubator. Maintain proper temperature and humidity levels as specified for the duck egg breed. Turning the eggs several times a day is crucial for successful hatching.

Artificial incubation allows you to hatch duck eggs without the presence of a broody duck. An incubator replicates the conditions needed for successful egg development and hatching. Maintaining consistent temperature and humidity levels is essential, as these factors influence embryo development and hatch rates. Different duck breeds may have specific requirements, so it's important to research and adjust settings accordingly. Turning the eggs multiple times daily prevents the embryo from sticking to the shell and promotes even development. Proper incubation techniques and careful monitoring and adjustments increase the chances of a successful hatch and healthy ducklings.

Feather Plucking

Q: Why do ducks sometimes pluck each other's feathers?

A: Feather plucking can result from overcrowding, stress, boredom, or nutritional deficiencies. To minimize feather plucking, make sure they have enough space, offer mental stimulation, and provide a balanced diet.

Various factors can cause feather plucking. Overcrowding in the coop or lack of space can lead to stress and aggression among ducks, resulting in feather plucking. Boredom and lack of mental stimulation can also contribute to this behavior. Ducks may engage in feather plucking if they have nutritional deficiencies or if their diet lacks essential nutrients. To prevent feather plucking, make sure that ducks have enough space to move around and interact without feeling crowded. Provide mental stimulation via toys, mirrors, and items to peck at to keep them engaged. Offering a balanced and nutritious diet tailored to their needs minimizes the risk of nutritional deficiencies that may lead to feather plucking.

Egg-Laying Patterns

Q: How often do ducks lay eggs?

A: Egg-laying frequency varies depending on factors such as breed, age, and lighting conditions. On average, ducks lay eggs every 24-26 hours. Some may lay consistently, while others may do so intermittently.

Ducks' egg-laying patterns can vary widely based on individual characteristics and environmental factors. Different breeds have different levels of egg production, with some being more prolific layers than others. Age also plays a role, as younger ducks tend to lay more eggs than older ones. Lighting conditions, particularly the number of daylight hours, influence egg production. Ducks typically lay eggs every 24-26 hours, with most laying early in the morning. However, some ducks may lay intermittently or take breaks from egg production. Monitoring egg-laying patterns and providing proper care, including suitable lighting, ensures optimal egg production and overall well-being.

Duck Sounds
Q: What do duck sounds mean?

A: Ducks communicate through various sounds. For example, females typically have a quack, while males make softer sounds. Quacking can indicate excitement, warning of danger, or simply socializing. Observing their behavior alongside sounds will help you understand their communication.

Ducks use vocalizations to communicate a range of messages and emotions. The quack is one of the most recognizable duck sounds and is typically associated with females. Male ducks often make softer sounds or whistles. Quacking can indicate excitement, such as when ducks are anticipating feeding or swimming. It can also serve as a warning signal to alert other ducks to potential danger. Ducks quack to maintain social connections and establish their presence within the flock. Observing their behavior and the context of their vocalizations will help you interpret their communication and understand their needs and feelings.

Molting
Q: How long does molting typically last?

A: Molting is the process of shedding old feathers and growing new ones. It can last several weeks to a couple of months. Provide proper nutrition and care during this time to support healthy feather regrowth.

Molting typically occurs annually and lasts from several weeks to a few months. During this time, ducks may look scruffy, and their egg production may decrease or cease temporarily. Molting requires significant energy, so providing a balanced and nutrient-rich diet is crucial to support healthy feather regrowth. Ducks may be more susceptible to stress and predation during molting, so make sure they have a safe and comfortable environment during this period. Once molting is complete, ducks will have fresh feathers that contribute to their overall health and appearance.

Duck Health and Medications
Q: Can you use medications on ducks that are intended for chickens?

A: Some safe medications for chickens may not be suitable for ducks. Always consult a poultry veterinarian before administering any medications to ensure proper dosage and effectiveness.

While chickens and ducks are both poultry, they have distinct physiological differences that can impact how they metabolize medications. Medications that are safe for chickens may not necessarily be safe or effective for ducks. Some may have different dosages, withdrawal periods, or potential side effects when used in ducks. Consulting a poultry veterinarian with experience in duck care is essential. A professional can provide guidance on appropriate treatments and dosages to ensure the health and well-being of your ducks.

Duck Behavior
Q: Why do ducks shake their heads in the water?

A: Ducks shake their heads in the water to clean their bills, eyes, and nostrils. This behavior helps remove dirt and debris, keeping their sensitive areas clean.

Ducks shake their heads as a natural behavior to maintain hygiene and comfort. When they do it in the water, they're cleaning their bills, eyes, and nostrils. They use their bills to forage for food and interact with their environment, so keeping them clean is important for overall health. Head shaking helps remove dirt, debris, and any foreign particles that may have accumulated. By observing this behavior, you can witness ducks' natural self-care routines and their adaptations for staying clean and healthy.

Duck Adoption
Q: Can you adopt or rescue ducks?

A: Yes, you can adopt or rescue ducks in need. Contact animal shelters, rescue organizations, or farm animal sanctuaries to inquire about adopting ducks. Make sure you can provide the appropriate care and living conditions before adopting.

Adopting or rescuing ducks can be a rewarding experience, but it requires careful consideration and preparation. If you want to provide a home for ducks in need, contact local animal shelters, rescue organizations, or farm animal sanctuaries. Due to various circumstances, such as abandonment or owner surrender, these organizations may have ducks available for adoption. You need to have the necessary resources, space, and knowledge to provide proper care. Ducks have specific needs, and it's important to create a suitable and safe environment that meets their requirements for housing, nutrition, and overall well-being.

These frequently asked questions provide valuable insights into the world of duck-keeping. By understanding and addressing these topics, you'll be better equipped to provide optimal care for your ducks and create a fulfilling and enriching experience for both you and your feathered companions.

Conclusion

There are so many reasons to consider opting for ducks over chickens or even alongside them. Ducks are known for their friendly nature, and caring for them can bring a lot of enjoyment. However, you should understand the responsibilities that come with duck care and what you should and shouldn't do.

Here are some key takeaways: Ducks don't require an elaborate shelter. They prefer a shelter with a bit of breeze and some moisture. It also needs to be predator-proof because of the many potential threats ducks face. Additionally, it should ideally be at ground level or close to it, as most ducks are uncomfortable with elevation.

Ducks need water, both for drinking and swimming. Creating a small pond is not necessary. As long as ducks can swim in a circle, they'll be content spending a significant part of their day doing so.

When selecting a duck type, choose one that suits your needs and is manageable for you. While getting fresh eggs daily is rewarding, keep in mind that two people with just four ducks could yield up to 800 eggs annually.

Caring for and interacting with ducks can be enjoyable, but it's a commitment that requires proper knowledge of feeding and care. This guide provides you with enough information to help you create a suitable habitat for your ducks, ensuring their well-being and happiness. Start small, especially if you're raising ducks for your personal use. If you have access to clean water nearby, your ducks can thrive.

Remember that even the quietest ducks can generate some noise and tend to be early risers. If you have neighbors, consider their comfort. Additionally, make sure to check with local authorities to confirm whether you're allowed to keep ducks and if there are any limits on the number you can keep.

On the flip side, ducks have charming personalities. They're curious, affectionate, and can become quite attached to their human caregivers. You're in for a treat if you're raising them for eggs. Duck eggs are larger and richer than chicken eggs, making them a prized ingredient in the kitchen. Plus, ducks are nature's pest control experts. They'll happily munch on slugs, snails, and various insects, which can help keep your garden pest-free. They also offer the bonus of feathers and down, which can be harvested for various craft projects or even sold. Beyond the practical benefits, raising ducks can deepen your connection to the natural world. It's a hands-on way to appreciate the cycles of life, the changing seasons, and the simple joys of outdoor living.

Here's another book by Dion Rosser that you might like

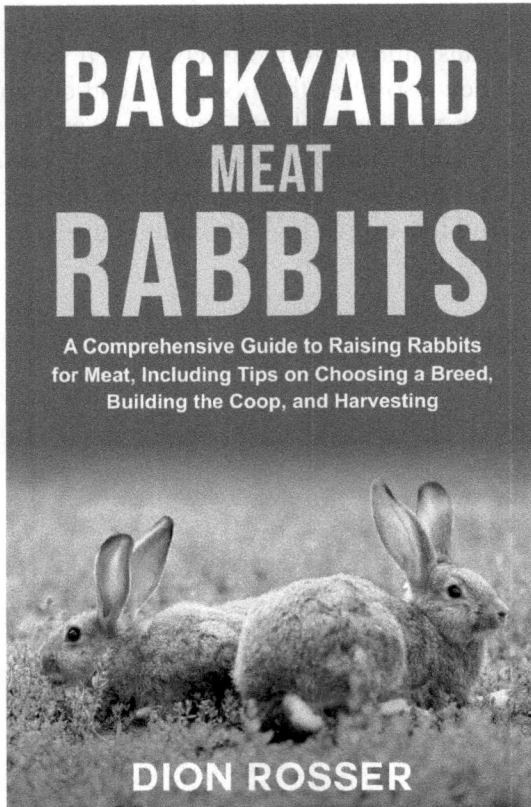

References

(N.d.). Bothellwa.gov. https://www.bothellwa.gov/561/Dont-Feed-the-Birds#:~:text=A%3A%20Ducks%20are%20natural%20foragers,plants%2C%20crustaceans%2C%20and%20more.

(N.d.). Veterinariadigital.com. https://www.veterinariadigital.com/en/articulos/main-challenges-in-duck-production/

(N.d.-a). Pethelpful.com. https://pethelpful.com/birds/Keeping-Pet-Ducks-and-Geese

(N.d.-b). Zendesk.com. https://meyerhatchery.zendesk.com/hc/en-us/articles/5316673386509-Raising-Ducks-for-Meat#:~:text=For%20the%20first%204%20weeks,not%20gain%20weight%20as%20efficiently.

12 reasons why duck eggs are better than chicken eggs. (2019, November 12). Fresh Eggs Daily® with Lisa Steele. https://www.fresheggsdaily.blog/2019/11/duck-eggs-vs-chicken-eggs-12-reasons.html

Accetta-Scott, A. (2021, October 27). Selecting the best ducks for eggs. Backyard Poultry. https://backyardpoultry.iamcountryside.com/poultry-101/selecting-the-best-ducks-for-eggs/

Addison, J. (2023, May 2). Feeding Ducks: The best food to keep ducks healthy & happy. Birds & Wetlands. https://birdsandwetlands.com/feeding-ducks/

Affeld, M. (2019, November 21). 10 delectable duck egg recipes. Insteading. https://insteading.com/blog/duck-egg-recipes/

Aktar, W., Sengupta, D., & Chowdhury, A. (2009). Impact of pesticides use in agriculture: their benefits and hazards. Interdisciplinary Toxicology, 2(1), 1–12. https://doi.org/10.2478/v10102-009-0001-7

American Pekin duck characteristics, origin, uses. (2021, May 31). ROYS FARM. https://www.roysfarm.com/pekin-duck/

Ariane Helmbrecht. (n.d.). Presswarehouse.com. https://styluspub.presswarehouse.com/browse/author/ff544176-aca6-4453-8b46-b9c9b67db340/Helmbrecht-Ariane

Aylesbury duck characteristics, origin & uses info. (2021, May 31). ROYS FARM. https://www.roysfarm.com/aylesbury-duck/

Aylesbury ducks: Complete breed guide. (n.d.). Fowl Guide. https://fowlguide.com/aylesbury-ducks/

Backyard Sidekick. (2022, October 6). Why do ducks quack? The various meanings of duck quacks. Backyard Sidekick. https://backyardsidekick.com/why-do-ducks-quack-the-various-meanings-of-duck-quacks/

Badgett, B. (2019, August 2). Duck habitat safety – what are some plants ducks can't eat. Gardening Know How. https://www.gardeningknowhow.com/garden-how-to/beneficial/plants-ducks-cant-eat.htm

Barnes, A. (2019, May 15). Daily diet, treats, and supplements for ducks. The Open Sanctuary Project; The Open Sanctuary Project, Inc. https://opensanctuary.org/daily-diet-treats-and-supplements-for-ducks/

Batres-Marquez, S.P. (2017, June 29). U.S. duck production and exports. Iowafarmbureau.com. https://www.iowafarmbureau.com/Article/US-Duck-Production-and-Exports

Bauer, E. (n.d.). Chocolate Mousse. Simply Recipes. https://www.simplyrecipes.com/recipes/chocolate_mousse/

Bethany. (2021, August 30). Raising baby ducks for beginners. Homesteading Where You Are. https://www.homesteadingwhereyouare.com/2021/08/30/raising-baby-ducks-for-beginners/

Bethany. (2022, February 4). All about niacin for ducks: What you should know. Homesteading Where You Are. https://www.homesteadingwhereyouare.com/2022/02/03/niacin-for-ducks/

Brahlek, A. (n.d.). A guide to the ideal diet for backyard ducks. Grubblyfarms.com. https://grubblyfarms.com/blogs/the-flyer/backyard-ducks-diet

Campbell, V. (2015, January 20). How to recognize duck courtship displays. All About Birds. https://www.allaboutbirds.org/news/what-to-watch-for-duck-courtship-video/

Can ducks eat chicken feed? Duck feeding 101. (2020, August 22). Rural Living Today. https://rurallivingtoday.com/backyard-chickens-roosters/can-ducks-eat-chicken-feed/

Chaussee, R. (n.d.). Amino acid nutrition in ducks. Org.Br. http://www.facta.org.br/wpc2012-cd/pdfs/plenary/Ariane_Helmbrecht.pdf

Chiou, J. (2021, September 16). Caramelized apple French toast. Table for Two® by Julie Chiou; Table for Two. https://www.tablefortwoblog.com/caramelized-apple-french-toast/

Commercial feeds. (2012, July 24). Horse Sport. https://horsesport.com/magazine/nutrition/commercial-feeds/

Cosgrove, N. (2022, August 5). Indian runner duck: Pictures, info, traits & care guide. Pet Keen. https://petkeen.com/indian-runner-duck/

DeVore, S. (2020, May 3). Duck breeds. Farminence. https://farminence.com/duck-breeds/

Dickson, P. (2022, October 1). Do ducks purr? Bird noises & interesting facts. Pet Keen. https://petkeen.com/do-ducks-purr/

Diet requirements for backyard ducks - A comprehensive guide. (2023, February 23). Sharpes Stock Feeds; Sharpes Stockfeed. https://www.stockfeed.co.nz/resources/poultry-feed/ducks-diet-requirements/

Dodrill, T. (2021, December 10). Duck language: How to interpret duck behavior. New Life On A Homestead. https://www.newlifeonahomestead.com/duck-language-and-behavior/

Duck egg production, lighting, and incubation. (2021). Gov.au. https://www.dpi.nsw.gov.au/animals-and-livestock/poultry-and-birds/species/duck-raising/egg-production

Duck eggs —. (n.d.). Orange Star Farm. https://www.orangestarfarm.com/duck-eggs

Duck health care. (2020, February 13). Cornell University College of Veterinary Medicine. https://www.vet.cornell.edu/animal-health-diagnostic-center/programs/duck-research-lab/health-care

Duck nutrition. (2020, February 17). Cornell University College of Veterinary Medicine. https://www.vet.cornell.edu/animal-health-diagnostic-center/programs/duck-research-lab/duck-nutrition

Emily. (2022, April 22). Duck egg quiche. This Healthy Table. https://thishealthytable.com/blog/duck-egg-quiche/

Feed mixers for cattle, poultry & Co – amixon® blog. (n.d.). Amixon.com. https://www.amixon.com/en/blog/feed-mixers

Feed supplements poultry shellgrit, Packaging Type: Bags. (n.d.). Indiamart.com. https://www.indiamart.com/proddetail/shellgrit-10716078848.html

Feeding ducks. (n.d.). Ncsu.edu. https://poultry.ces.ncsu.edu/backyard-flocks-eggs/other-fowl/feeding-ducks/

Ferraro-Fanning, A. (2022, June 21). Duck-safe plants and weeds from the garden. Backyard Poultry. https://backyardpoultry.iamcountryside.com/poultry-101/weeding-the-garden-and-duck-safe-plants/

Fraser, C. (2022, May 17). Pekin duck (American Pekin): Pictures, info, traits, & care guide. Pet Keen. https://petkeen.com/pekin-duck/

Girl, L. E. D. (2012, May 31). The beginner's guide to hatching duck eggs. Fresh Eggs Daily® with Lisa Steele. https://www.fresheggsdaily.blog/2012/05/great-eggscape-too-hatching-duck-eggs.html

Greer, T. (2020, July 6). How much protein do ducks really need? Morning Chores. https://morningchores.com/protein-requirements-for-ducks/

Gregory. (2021, July 23). Duck eggs: Taste, preparation, shelf life, and more. Fowl Guide. https://fowlguide.com/duck-eggs-taste-preparation/

HappyChicken. (2020, September 26). Interpreting duck behavior. The Happy Chicken Coop. https://www.thehappychickencoop.com/interpreting-duck-behavior/

HappyChicken. (2021, October 12). Pekin duck breed: Everything you need to know. The Happy Chicken Coop. https://www.thehappychickencoop.com/pekin-duck-breed-everything-you-need-to-know/

HappyChicken. (2022, March 2). Ducks need water. The Happy Chicken Coop. https://www.thehappychickencoop.com/do-ducks-need-water-what-you-should-know/

HappyChicken. (2022, March 4). Best meat duck breeds. The Happy Chicken Coop. https://www.thehappychickencoop.com/best-meat-duck-breeds/

Health & Social Services. (n.d.). Duck. Gov.Nt.Ca. https://www.hss.gov.nt.ca/en/services/nutritional-food-fact-sheet-series/duck

Henke, J. (2020, August 3). Should you wash eggs or not? Successful Farming. https://www.agriculture.com/podcast/living-the-country-life-radio/should-you-wash-eggs-or-not

Herlihy, S. (2022, June 6). Khaki Campbell duck: Breed info, pictures, traits & care guide. Pet Keen. https://petkeen.com/khaki-campbell-duck/

Hess, T., & Griffler, M. (2018, April 3). Potential duck health challenges. The Open Sanctuary Project; The Open Sanctuary Project, Inc. https://opensanctuary.org/common-duck-health-issues/

Hess, T., & Griffler, M. (2018, March 7). Welcome to waterfowl: The new duck arrival guide. The Open Sanctuary Project; The Open Sanctuary Project, Inc. https://opensanctuary.org/new-duck-arrival-guide/

Hess, T., & Griffler, M. (2023, May 26). How to conduct a duck health check. The Open Sanctuary Project; The Open Sanctuary Project, Inc. https://opensanctuary.org/how-to-conduct-a-duck-health-examination/

Holley, M. (2020, April 19). Raising ducks - pros and cons of backyard ducks. Outdoor Happens. https://www.outdoorhappens.com/raising-ducks-pros-and-cons-of-backyard-ducks/

How do ducks communicate? (2019, November 23). Sciencing; Leaf Group. https://sciencing.com/ducks-communicate-4574402.html

How to store duck eggs (step-by-step guide). (2022, October 2). Homestead Crowd | Homesteading, Gardening, Raising Animals Tips; Homestead Crowd. https://homesteadcrowd.com/how-to-store-duck-eggs/

Human-imprinting in birds and the importance of surrogacy. (n.d.). Wildlifecenter.org. https://www.wildlifecenter.org/human-imprinting-birds-and-importance-surrogacy

Indian Runner duck characteristics, uses & origin. (2021, May 31). ROYS FARM. https://www.roysfarm.com/indian-runner-duck/

Jagdish. (2022, August 10). How to start duck farming from scratch: A detailed guide for beginners. Agri Farming. https://www.agrifarming.in/how-to-start-duck-farming-from-scratch-a-detailed-guide-for-beginners

Khaki Campbell ducks: Characteristics, origin, uses. (2021, May 31). ROYS FARM. https://www.roysfarm.com/khaki-campbell-duck/

Kim, J. (2022a, August 26). Muscovy duck: Facts, uses, origins & characteristics (with pictures). Pet Keen. https://petkeen.com/muscovy-duck/

Kross, J. (2022). Waterfowl vocalizations. Ducks.org. https://www.ducks.org/conservation/waterfowl-research-science/waterfowl-vocalizations

Lazzari, Z. (2011, May 30). When & how to collect duck eggs. Pets on Mom.com; It Still Works. https://animals.mom.com/when-how-to-collect-duck-eggs-12546035.html

Lee, A. (2023, May 28). Decoding duck behavior: A guide for duck owners. Farmhouse Guide; April Lee. https://farmhouseguide.com/decoding-duck-behavior/

Lee. (2020, October 15). How to butcher a duck – a step-by-step picture tutorial. Lady Lee's Home; Lady Lees Home. https://ladyleeshome.com/how-to-butcher-a-duck/

Lesley, C. (n.d.). Hatching duck eggs: Complete 28-day incubation guide. Chickensandmore.com. https://www.chickensandmore.com/incubating-duck-eggs/

Lesley, C. (n.d.-a). Indian runner Ducks for beginners (the complete care sheet). Chickensandmore.com. https://www.chickensandmore.com/indian-runner-duck/

Lesley, C. (n.d.-b). Khaki Campbell duck: Care guide, size, eggs, and more.... Chickensandmore.com. https://www.chickensandmore.com/khaki-campbell-duck/

Lie-Nielsen, K. (2020, September 7). Ducks & geese are great permaculture livestock. Hobby Farms. https://www.hobbyfarms.com/ducks-and-geese-great-permaculture-livestock/

Liz. (2016, May 4). How to make a duck house. The Cape Coop. https://thecapecoop.com/make-duck-house/

Liz. (2016, September 28). Understanding backyard duck behavior. The Cape Coop. https://thecapecoop.com/understanding-backyard-duck-behavior/

Mallard duck nests. (n.d.). Wildlifecenter.org. https://www.wildlifecenter.org/mallard-duck-nests

Mallard life history. (n.d.). Allaboutbirds.org. https://www.allaboutbirds.org/guide/Mallard/lifehistory

Mccune, K. (2021, May 16). What is the best bedding to use for ducklings? Family Farm Livestock. https://familyfarmlivestock.com/what-is-the-best-bedding-to-use-for-ducklings/

Molly. (2022, July 19). Indian Runner ducks: Personality, appearance, and care tips. Know Your Chickens. https://www.knowyourchickens.com/indian-runner-ducks/

Muscovy duck: Characteristics, diet, uses, facts. (2021, May 31). ROYS FARM. https://www.roysfarm.com/muscovy-duck/

New Life on a Homestead. (2022, November 3). Top 10 duck keeping questions answered. Backyard Poultry. https://backyardpoultry.iamcountryside.com/poultry-101/top-10-duck-raising-questions-answered/

(n.d.). HGTV; Discovery UK. https://www.hgtv.com/outdoors/gardens/animals-and-wildlife/plants-toxic-to-backyard-ducks

Perez, S. (n.d.). Keeping Pet Ducks: Ducklings, Imprinting, and Ethical Treatment. Pethelpful.com. https://pethelpful.com/birds/Keeping-Pet-Ducks-and-Geese

Phillips, E. (2022, January 18). How to care for ducklings. Backyard Poultry. https://backyardpoultry.iamcountryside.com/poultry-101/how-to-care-for-ducklings/

Pierce, R. (2020, August 12). How to introduce new ducks to the flock. The Homesteading Hippy. https://thehomesteadinghippy.com/introducing-ducks-to-the-flock/

Pierce, R. (2022, September 17). Common duck diseases and how to prevent them. The Happy Chicken Coop. https://www.thehappychickencoop.com/duck-diseases/

Pierce, R. (2022, September 30). Free-range ducks: Pros and cons. The Happy Chicken Coop. https://www.thehappychickencoop.com/free-range-ducks-pros-and-cons/

Pierce, R. (2022a, August 10). Aylesbury ducks - the ultimate duck breed guide. The Happy Chicken Coop. https://www.thehappychickencoop.com/aylesbury-duck/

Poindexter, J. (2016, August 28). 10 important things to consider when building a duck coop. Morning Chores. https://morningchores.com/duck-coop-considerations/

Raising meat ducks in small and backyard flocks. (n.d.). Extension.org. https://poultry.extension.org/articles/poultry-management/raising-meat-ducks-in-small-and-backyard-flocks/

Reddy. (2023, March 10). Frequently Asked Questions About Duck Farming. AgriculturalMagazine. https://agriculturalmagazine.com/frequently-asked-questions-about-duck-farming/

Rice and duck farming as a means for contributing to climate change adaptation and mitigation. (n.d.). Fao.org. https://www.fao.org/family-farming/detail/en/c/1618289/

Sachdev, P. (n.d.). Are there health benefits of duck? WebMD. https://www.webmd.com/diet/health-benefits-duck

Sam, & February 1. (2020, February 1). Duck egg carbonara. Our Modern Kitchen. https://www.ourmodernkitchen.com/duck-egg-carbonara/

Sargent, A. (2020, November 28). Everything you ever wanted to know about duck eggs. Crooked Chimney Farm, LLC. https://crookedchimneyfarm.com/blogs/chickens-ducks/everything-you-ever-wanted-to-know-about-duck-eggs

Shaw, H. (2020, November 2). Duck fried rice. Hunter Angler Gardener Cook. https://honest-food.net/duck-fried-rice-recipe/

Shelton, L. (2023, March 13). Duck coops: 15 tips to design the perfect coop for your ducks. AgronoMag. https://agronomag.com/duck-coops/

Signs of malnutrition in birds. (2022, October 8). Petindiaonline.com. https://www.petindiaonline.com/story-details.php?ref=160503223

Steele, L. (2022, December 19). Types of ducks for eggs, meat, and pest control. Backyard Poultry.

https://backyardpoultry.iamcountryside.com/poultry-101/types-of-ducks-for-eggs-meat-and-pest-control/

Stockman, F. (2019, June 18). People are taking emotional support animals everywhere. States are cracking down. The New York Times. https://www.nytimes.com/2019/06/18/us/emotional-support-animal.html

Stone, K. (2019, November 18). Commercial vs. Home mixed feed: Helpful answers for you. Stone Family Farmstead; Kristi Stone. https://www.stonefamilyfarmstead.com/commercial-vs-home-mixed-feed/

The DOs and DON'ts of feeding ducks. (n.d.). Friscolibrary.com. https://friscolibrary.com/blogs/post/the-dos-and-donts-of-feeding-ducks/

The Happy Chicken Coop. (2022, September 26). Muscovy duck: Eggs, facts, care guide, and more. The Happy Chicken Coop. https://www.thehappychickencoop.com/muscovy-duck/

The hidden lives of ducks and geese. (2010, June 22). PETA. https://www.peta.org/issues/animals-used-for-food/factory-farming/ducks-geese/hidden-lives-ducks-geese/

Thrifty Homesteader. (2016, June 23). Want eggs? Get ducks! The Thrifty Homesteader. https://thriftyhomesteader.com/want-eggs-get-ducks/

von Frank, A. (2022, August 30). 11 things you should know before raising ducks. Tyrant Farms. https://www.tyrantfarms.com/10-things-you-should-know-before-you-get-ducks/

von Frank, A. (2022, November 1). Duck eggs vs. chicken eggs: how do they compare? Tyrant Farms. https://www.tyrantfarms.com/5-things-you-didnt-know-about-duck-eggs/

von Frank, A. (2023, February 2). Are ducks dirty? Top tips for keeping your duck areas clean. Tyrant Farms. https://www.tyrantfarms.com/are-ducks-dirty-top-tips-for-keeping-duck-areas-clean/

What do ducks eat? Tips and best practices. (n.d.). Purinamills.com. https://www.purinamills.com/chicken-feed/education/detail/what-do-ducks-eat-tips-and-best-practices-for-feeding-backyard-ducks

What ducks and geese are good for foraging? (n.d.). Metzerfarms.com. https://www.metzerfarms.com/blog/what-ducks-and-geese-are-good-for-foraging.html

What should I feed my ducks? (2018, November 9). Org.au. https://kb.rspca.org.au/knowledge-base/what-should-i-feed-my-ducks/

When do you need a vet? (2016, July 7). Raising-ducks.com. https://www.raising-ducks.com/when-do-you-need-a-vet/

www.ingramcontent.com/pod-product-compliance
Lightning Source LLC
Chambersburg PA
CBHW070811300326
41914CB00054B/766